PEACE,

A PANACEA TO NATION BUILDING:

Counselling, A Tool for Effective Leadership.

Your #1 guiding book for effective leadership

Akanni Olajide Kwam

E-mail: instincthillincorporated@gmail.com

Contents

Foreword	i
Preface	iii
Chapter 1: Establishment of Nation state	1
Chapter 2: Governance, A major drive to Nation building	25
Chapter 3: Public Policy and Nation Building	60
Chapter 4: Conflicts, Revolutions, and Nation Building	83
Chapter 5: Leadership, The Key to Transformation	108
Chapter 6: Values, The Component to Enhancing Nation Building	133
Chapter 7: Establishing Societal Enlightenment to Aid Good Governance	160
Chapter 8: Influencing Nation Building With Value Orientation	171

Foreword

Leadership as an embodiment of character is interjectory in individual trait. The instinctual abilities possessed by everyone unconsciously and exhibited in a variety of endeavors that actually and gradually positioned to leadership role with progression from accumulated experiences with leadership attributes garnered within necessitated timeframe. As a structure of functionality, primarily propel by composure of establishments to an organized entity where everyone within the domain of the establishment act in accordance to the objective and purpose of the organizational goals that is mostly driven with visionary leaders.

The world certainly is a replica of the leaders and neither do nations fall short of this, keeping a nation together is a continual process of governance to ensure continuous stability in its entity which is enhanced by peaceful co-existence of the people. The essence of governance is the sustainability of the nation that is foster by peace, and beholding peace to have an entity called nation is the responsibility of governance. But what makes the structure of governance is far more important than the system of governance itself. The structure of governance is a clear cut to the ascension to leadership positions that narrate individual's behavioral expectations for leadership roles that is expected to impact in the wellbeing of the nation; whereas, the system of governance is a pattern to conduct the affairs of a country.

Leadership roles are significant to sustain a nation, some nations have drifted apart to annexation due to a faulty structural pattern of governance that does not properly outline the procedure to ascension to leadership positions which alongside result to deficiency in behavioral expectation and experiences to function effectively within the capacities of the positions. Leadership, as a major factor that propel peace, has also been responsible for creating discord amidst the people and truncating peaceful co-existence in nations.

This Book; Peace, A Panacea to Nation Building: Counselling, A Tool for Effective Leadership. Is conceived and regarded as a guideline for effective leadership irrespective of the establishment that enhances leader's foresight and cognitive abilities to be proactive during decision making process in the function of their roles.

Sulaimon Olajide Kwam

Chief Executive/Founder

Instincthill Incorporated

Preface

This book focuses on the necessary parameters required towards nation building, it considers the administrative style of affairs as a major pattern and factor that ignite nation building, it weighs the leadership elites roles in the development of a nation and/with increasing necessities on needs to collaborate with the counseling professions in involvement in administrative system with leading elites towards making appropriate decision making and in proffering solutions to the increasing societal problems that is factor to denigrating the values of some nations towards growth. With the eccentric nature of the profession in endowed knowledge in virtually all human facets, it is a discipline required to be integrated in any pattern of administrative system for utmost attainment of purpose.

Sulaimon Olajide Kwam

Chief Executive/Founder

Instincthill Incorporated

PEACE A PANACEA TO NATION BUILDING

INTRODUCTION

Nation building is the rudiment of agitation for the establishment of a common identity that emanates from particular group of people whose interest are identical on having a stand which the peoples' right and authority confines upon. The rights and authority cover the landscape where the people exercise their authority over the geographical entity into making it a nation of taste.

But what makes a nation!? This is obviously a creation of birth. The procreation of people that multiples into numbers transcends and transgresses within its domains and beyond in the process of getting along with life which is the first stage of conformity to group/s people aligns to that forms the initial basis of self-awareness and societal identification. Time, is the mystery of man, and it present itself in the condition of man at the time. What once perceived small turns big, the expanding population of humans increases the intellectual capacities of its functionality and in the process creating a diverse multicultural and ethnical societies where people now find it a necessity to relate and interaction with differs ethnical establishments which alongside compounds the complexity of self and societal identification as groups get interwoven. This to large scale, further pluralized the complexity of identification through creating territorial control over the landscape for the community to establish authority for a place of their own whom its inhabitants are entitled to. With this, we can justify ethnic linings to nations due to shared common interests, values, cultures and traditions of the people and the territorial landscape it occupied.

Establishment of Nation State

A nation state can be regarded as a large territorial composition comprising confederating unit of groups with similarities and interest that establish a constituted terrain governed by its collective ideas (Akanni 2022). It is the togetherness of groups who seeks to create a territorial balance in its affairs from external behavioral interference and affluence and crave for a common identity that defines the nationness and defends the people's interest. On this note, they are a grounded consensus for desires of shared prosperity and establishment of a commonwealth that frequently manages and channel its resources to effective use for growth of the nation-state.

The antecedents of nationness at its emergence entails agitation for self-governance through the process of self-determination that is mostly formed from the basis of a common stance by the collective inhabitants whom initially practices communal establishment of territorial administration; with limitation on the activities on growth to the terrain. A nation in isolation is a nation vulnerable to external invasion and interference, more so, a communal establishment that shares borders with opposing community often poses threat to peaceful co-existences creating the scenario of tension for possible invasion that emanates from violation/trespasses on borderlines. And since a community is an extension of an initial society, to eliminate the threat from whom it differs, then allies with immediate community is pertinent that give rise to forming of forces and increasingly establishment of a stronger borderlines with neighbors. Ironically, this is the first formation for willingness to self-determination towards strengthening nation's abilities for growth and defense that was once gullible and difficult to attain functioning as a singular community. From streams of nation-state creation, the peculiarities have been a relatively shared similarities in languages, values, cultures and traditions and the willingness for self-governance for the vast territorial landscape. The first line of nations has its turns of flesh with creation, which is having the approximately required inhabitants with the appropriate behavioral expression towards nationhood. This is the foundation that upholds the nations' interest as it reveals the philosophical principles for its sovereignty; which mostly are the sacrifices and physical dedications from nationalism that result to establishment of a sovereign state.

The British commonwealth is regarded as the earliest instance of nation building through declaration of an Act by the vested authority of the Parliament and Council of State on 19 May 1649 after the end of the Second English Civil War affirming England and Wales as a republic, the declaration precedes beyond the year due to continua war with Ireland and Scotland. And in 1653, a dissolution of the initial 1649 Parliamentary Act took effect, afterwards, the Army Council adopted the instrument of Government which made a united Commonwealth of England, Wales, Scotland and Ireland. Due to Oliver Cromwell death as the Lord Protector of the United Commonwealth in 1659; the protectorate parliament was dissolved, recalled and started the process that led to restoration of the monarchy in 1660 and recognition of the throne as Head of State.

Another event that shaped the formation of a nation is the French revolution that began in 1789 and ended in late 1790s with the ascent of Napoleon Bonaparte.

During this period the French citizens radically altered the political landscape by uprooting centuries-old institutions of the monarchy and the feudal system which was caused by disgust with the French aristocracy and the economic policies of King Louis XVI. The French Revolution helped to shape modern democracies by showing the power inherent in the will of the people. While France is the first to embrace democracy as a nation from imperialism, America is the first to attain Independence from imperialism via war.

The American Revolution was an important global event in the formation of a sovereign state. An epic struggle waged between 1765 and 1783 when 13 of Britain's North America colonies rejected its imperial rule. The disagreement grew from opposition to taxes levied by the British monarchy and Parliament which triggered defiant acts and punitive laws that led to rebellion. The enactment of tax policy on products without representatives from the colonies was tagged tyrannical. The revolutionary war entails series of engagement at the battlegrounds with nations such as France and Spain joining to aid the colonies in the war with Britain. As the war broke out, the governments of each colony formally declared their independence, throwing a bait to seizing the opportunity of purpose to win its sovereignty which alongside led to adoption of measures not losing the battle. The surrender of a faction of the British army convinced the British government to negotiate an end to the war and recognize America's independence. The treaty of Paris was signed on September 3, 1783, which marked the end of the revolutionary War.

The facts acknowledged from formation of the first generational nations are: -

- The desire for reforms of the administrative systems
- The desire to integrate the inhabitants as integral part of the modern world
- And the desire to enhance peaceful co-existence of inhabitants by enacting policies that check and balances activities within confined territorial landscape.

From all indications, nation building can only be attained through sustenance of peace. And peace on its part is enhanced by the people by embracing the dividends of governance.

The skepticism of peace is war, and wars does not revolve without conflicts. The establishment of nations are basis on territorial controls. The early years of formation of nations have no prior establishment of treaties or policies adopted by a united front binding the existences and functionalities of nation state, but with embrace of civility through the process of accords withs warring parties in territorial disputes from prolonged years of rifts brought about the necessity for enacting treaties that normalizes the affairs of nations in their confined territorial landscapes. The formations of nations are historically linked to Westphalain peace treaties of 1648 that made an end to both the thirty years' war in the Roman Empire and the Eighty years' war between Spain and the Dutch, with Spain formally recognizing the independence of the Dutch Republic. The recognition of nations pave ways for diplomacy in the global scene through the establishment of organizations that balances bilateral activities of member state. This purpose was initially implemented by intermediaries that mediate between nations during conflict resolutions.

While the 17th and 18th centuries were engulfed in wars and formations of nations by imperialism in its colonies particularly in the Northern and Southern America countries that led to recognition of independences. With the civility from past events, by 19th century the world should have been at peace. Instead, otherwise was the situation, Europe went agog with World War I between July 1914 and November 11, 1918. By the end of the war, over 17 million people was estimated to have been killed. The rationale behind engagement of nations in the war is what should be justified, the precedents of wars that led to formations of most European nations and independences of North and South American Nations actually yields to the establishment of Mutual Defense Alliances of nations for eventualities of battle. Over time, countries through Europe made mutual defense agreements. These treaties meant that if one country was attacked, allied countries were bound to defend them. Before World War I, the following alliances existed:

- Russia and Serbia
- Germany and Austria-Hungary
- France and Russia
- Britain and France and Belgium
- Japan and Britain

Prior to the War, Imperial nations were referred to by their Militarism and affluent of wealth. And these were the factors for territorial expansion and dominance. The territorial disputes of Bosnia which was part of Austria-Hungary and the attempt by Serbia to absorbed Bosnia and Herzegovina to her nation actually led to the World War I with the assassination of Archduke Franz Ferdinand of Austria-Hungary in June 1914 in Bosnia by Serbia nationalist named Gavrilo Princip. This assassination led to Austria-Hungary declaring war on Serbia. When Russia began to mobilize due to its alliance with Serbia, Germany declared war on Russia. Thus, began the expansion of the war to include all those involved in the mutual defense alliances. On the contrary, the imperial countries craved for opportunity to prove their military dominance and power which was building up prior to the war, and ceased the declaration of war by Austria-Hungary to engage in battlefront in claims of alliances that exist between countries instead of utilizing the treaties to mediate between the conflicting nations on the territorial disputes, and perhaps settled the assassination of the Austria-Hungary nationalist by a rival nationalist on a disputed territory before the event degenerated into war.

As it is that nation building in not only aligned to the formation of an independent entity as a country, but rather, the continuous process of collective responsibility of the inhabitants whom is constituted for her sustenance in its establishments. An affluent nation can easily be put to ruined through the event of war. So, nation building is likened to balancing peaceful atmosphere in the event of conflicts and disaster as this is what measures the strength of philosophical ideologies of the governed. With sound philosophical ideologies of governance, all situations posing as challenges would be rightly considered by its implications and impacts on the nation in decision making. This is what should have been at the forefront in the aftermaths effect from World War I; the end of war is not outright end of grudges that emanated in pre and post war scenarios, It's only a call-off from physical engagement, the psychological effect still ripples on and if not properly catered, the tendency of reoccurrence of the event is still attached to the event due to unresolved issues that led to the war. Else, World War II would not have taken place. Another calamitous event that befell the world from irrationality. The war was in many respects a continuation, after an uneasy 20years hiatus, of the disputes left unsettled by World War I. The conflict involved virtually every part of the world during the years 1939-1945. The principal belligerents were the Axis powers- Germany, Italy, and Japan and the Allies- France, Great Britain, the United States, the Soviet Union, and, China.

Peace and Nation Building

The essence of nation building is peace, no nation is built without strong a foundational structure on peace. All nations have it fair share of challenges that led to it formations, and the ability to properly navigate around issues are what distinguishes nations as entities. The process of formation are procedures adopted in resolution of compelling conflicts that emanates from the emergence of independent nations that portray as hindrances to enhancing peaceful co-existence and balancing inequalities that could springs from diversity to aim and establish an atmosphere where the people are inspired to pursue and support national development for the interest of the nation.

The engulfment of the early 19th century with two consecutive World War led the League of Nation to respond swiftly by creating a diplomatic forum that oversees the activities of global affairs through preventive measures which all independent nations are subjected to for bilateral relations; and putting in place a template where individual nation are guided by the code of conducts of international diplomacy in attempt to avert violation of territorial borders to enhance peace and avert scenarios that could lead to violence or war. It was apparent that the essence of war is needless and the aftermaths are mostly meant with compromises on established grounds with parties involved having to endure damages and implications of the war.

The United Nation as an international organization was founded in 1945 after the Second World War by 51 countries committed to maintaining international peace and security, developing friendly relations among nations and promoting social progress, better living standards and human rights. Its later expanse to 193 member states with a platform to express views through the General Assembly, the Security Council, the Economic and Social Council and other bodies and committees which virtually covers every aspect of the globe.

The formation process of the United Nation is aligned to the formation format of a nation. A nation is an embodiment of the territorial space with elements that most conjoined to be called an entity. The formation of an independent nation is guided by three basic principles which are considered as perspectives to be thoroughly examined in the creation of a nation state. These are what defines the pattern and structural establishment of the existence of the entity. The perspectives on which a nation is formed is classified in three categories: -

1.) **The pattern of the administrative systems** – It's the collective responsibilities of the inhabitants to select the pattern that properly balances ambiguities in its diversity in measures to avoid denigration of its existence towards national development and enhance peaceful coordination of its affairs. This is through assertion of constituted activities that yields the polity into national dynamism and pursue peaceful co-existence through perspectives asserted from policy makers that functions as conducts for the governed. It includes the procedure of power sharing and authority distribution to various governmental parastatals to perform in respective roles as recognized by the pattern being practiced. Succinctly, this is the role of culture and human interrelationship to generate a sense of hope and belonging that motivate the nation to move forward together, which consists combining intellectual forces that collectively propels the economic structure and peacebuilding for the wellbeing of the people.

2.) **Integration of the inhabitants as part of the modern world** – An ideal nation is birthed from the willingness to have an established territorial domain by its inhabitant which is realized through placement of necessary mechanism that foster national integration of the people in the polity. It is the political ideal that transpires in the people from the advancement in the polity into transforming an existing pattern of administration to a system where the core values of the people are nationalized as the purpose of governance and formation of a nation state. This has been the yardstick for formation of many independent nations; and its antecedent is from America after recognition as a nation was attained through waging of revolutionary war between 1765 and 1783 when 13 of Britain's North America colonies rejected its imperial rule. This is based on the disagreement that grew from opposition to taxes levied by the British monarchy and Parliament which triggered defiant acts against the law and led to rebellion. The people perceived the tax policy on products without representatives from the colonies as being tyrannical by the imperial rule which led to the revolutionary War and recognition of the America as an independent nation when the treaty of Paris was signed on September 3, 1783, which marked the end of the revolutionary War. The aftermath effect of the American revolutionary war also led to an event that altered the French sovereignty with a revolution that began in 1789 and ended in late 1790s with the ascent of Napoleon Bonaparte. During this period the French citizens radically altered the political landscape by uprooting centuries-old institutions of the monarchy and the feudal system which was caused by disgust with the French aristocracy and the economic policies of King Louis XVI. The

French Revolution helped to shape modern democracies by showing the power inherent in the will of the people.

3.) **Effecting and enhancing peaceful co-existence of inhabitants through policies that balances activities within confined territorial landscape** – The sovereignty of the people is the first founding principle of the nation which legitimize nation building with a people centric approach ascribed to it entity which is defined in terms of territories over which institutional authorities exercise legitimate control. Enhancing peaceful coexistence is the application of approaches to establishing and enforcing institutional instruments in form of constituted documents interpreted as policies safeguarding the security, internal peace, and enforcement of the policies for national development.

There was three great optimism worldwide about the possibility of lasting peace and there was confidence that the peace individual would shift resources from weaponry to efforts of peace and development. The agenda for peace became the UN umbrella for a broad, comprehensive strategy consisting of five pillars.

1.) **Preventive Diplomacy:** Which seeks to reduce the danger of violence and increase the prospects of peaceful settlement.

2.) **Peace enforcement:** This authorizes the UN to act with or without the consent of the warring parties involved in order to ensure compliance with a ceasefire mandated by the Security Council acting under the authority of Chapter VII of the UN Charter.

3.) **Peacemaking:** It is designed to bring hostile parties to agreement through peaceful means such as those found in Chapter VII of the UN Charter.

4.) **Peacekeeping:** This is established to deploy a United Nations presence in the field, hitherto with the consent of all the parties concerned; as a confidence building measures to monitor a truce between the parties while diplomats strive to negotiate a comprehensive peace or officials to implement an agreed peace.

5.) **Post-Conflict reconstruction:** This is often organized to foster economic and social cooperation with the purpose of building confidence among previously warring parties, developing the social, political, and economic infrastructure to prevent future violence, and laying the foundations for a durable peace.

This commitment to global peace was reinforced in 2005 by the adoption of a new international security and human rights norm called the Responsibility to Protect(R2P). R2P project was pushed for in the wake of the genocide in Rwanda where the world was watching without intervening. In cases of mass atrocities committed against populations whose national governments are unable and/or willing to protect them. The commitments of the international community were underpinned by the concept of human security, which had first been introduced in the Human Development report of 1994. The great appeal of the broad and inclusive Peace Agenda and the Concept of human security is their holistic approach: Peace and security are not understood merely as the absence of war; the ambition is to let people flourish and prosper.

The UN defines peace-building as 'A range of measures targeted to reduce the risk of lapsing into conflict by strengthening national capacities at all levels for conflicts management and to lay the foundation for sustainable peace and development. Peacemaking is the process that is necessary to end conflict and forge peace agreements on the other hand. It is used to promote a much too broad range of interventions, which creates confusion because it overlaps with activities that really belong to the nation-building process. It should also comprise a carefully prioritized, sequenced and relatively narrow set of activities aimed to achieving the above objectives. In line with this definition, the 2009 report of the Secretary General on peace-building identified five priority areas: -

1.) Support of basic safety and security
2.) Political Processes
3.) Provision of basic services
4.) Restoration of core government functions
5.) Economic Revitalization

These priority areas clearly overlap with the nation-building agenda. The UN notion of peace-building gives the impression that it is a continuation of peacemaking using the same conceptual framework and the same analysis of roles and responsibilities. Official peace agreement that ends the active conflict however, is just the first and limited step in the process. Official peace agreements are political outcomes of negotiations by parties who were unable to defeat the other. In peace agreement many issues remain unresolved, are postponed or only solved in procedural terms. Peacemaking requires a strong role by an external party (or parties) that has convening power to bring to bring the different warring groups to the negotiation table. The process of fostering meaningful social relations and social capital based on trust is part of a nation-building strategy.

In peace processes the first steps are taken in building the bridging side of social capital. Different groups meet each other, acknowledge the need to find ways for solving their problems other than war and are willing to listen to each other, even if they are still focused on how best to push their agenda through. This groundwork of bridging has to be present in order for the processes of nation-building to take off and become successful. Nation building is not a solution for conflict, it is a protective factor for countries to prevent relapse into conflict over and over again.

Peacemaking in terms of ending the conflicts is a prerequisite for any form of nation-building to begin. As long as conflict and war continue, neither process will be effective. A negotiated peace agreement that ends the active conflict however, is just the first and limited step in this process. Nation-building builds on the peacemaking efforts. Its purpose is to make the initial steps of a peace agreement more robust by transforming them from agreement -out-of-necessity and based on political calculations to a fundament of understanding and mutual respect that will come to underpin the sense of belonging and the social relations of the different groups.

Peace and nation are hereby interwoven, without peace no nation will be regarded as an entity. Peace therefore is the undertone of a nation that propels the existence of oneness and necessitates the attitude of togetherness towards reaching a collective objective. It is an essential ingredient in formation and sustenance of any setting that enhances human interaction, and it is pivotal for aiding progress in any establishment. Nation is likened to a peaceful atmosphere bond by regards and respect on its establishment with firmness on transparency as foundation upholding and guiding behavioral conducts within the terrain.

Nations are territory confined in its identified landscape. And territory is with no establishment of purpose or values, or meaning if no livelihood occurs within; but established with the aim to be occupied for livelihood for it to attain a meaning. Mans' quest for sustainability makes it mandatory to converse with the environment by utilizing availed resources and according it with his knowledge and skills to meet and address his needs. As it relate with the obvious that a place where no livelihood occurs is no organize setting to enact laws that guide the activities and appropriate conducts expected to be obliged by individuals who choose to reside therein to sustain and maintain orderliness so as not to exceed the threshold expected within the confined establishment of the territory in the process of interaction with the various components.

Akanni (2020) posits that a nation is a collective of geographical entities that necessarily do not share common values, but share common desire to have all elements in various constituents attain utmost purpose with judicious utility of its resources for the betterment of the people. It is a consensus by the people to come together, to understand and absorb the differences between lines and form a territory identified as a nation that accommodates respective values, beliefs and equality for all. It is with this formation that mutual understanding attunes amidst the people which is the yardstick for continuity as a nation because without regards for each other, no nation can sustain its existence.

Features of a Nation

1. **Common Descent:**

People inhabiting a nation usually have a common origin and descent.

2. **Geographical Boundaries:**
A nation which is at the same time a state has clear-cut geographical boundaries. People that form a nation may live within a defined territory.

3. **Government:**
Most nation-states have their own political institutions that come together to form a government.

4. **Common Language:**
Inhabitants of a nation have a common language.

5. **Infrequent Internal Ethnic Conflicts:**
One other unique feature of a nation is the fact that conflicts and disagreements are not as pronounced as is the case in diverse and heterogeneous states.

6. **Common Religion:**
People inhabiting the nation tend to have common religions

7. **Same Cultural Practices:**
People of a nation usually have common customary or traditional practices. This is perhaps one of the most striking characteristics of a nation.

The basis for governance takes place to foster prosperity, growth and development within the territory by establishing administrative system accepted by majority through a process of selection that determines the pattern and how to govern the affairs of its entity. When a nation strive, it is purported that the political will of the administrative system match and cater for the will of the people; and when the need of the people are meant, rapport foster as the outcome of a good synergy between the governed and the political entity which signals strong co-existence between the people, the territory, the law, and nature. The strength of nations is measured by the ability to adequately govern the affairs with suiting formulated laws and policies to check and channel its resources and people towards the path to growth, to this regard, it is imperative to note that:

(i) Governance
(ii) Leadership
(iii) Values
(iv) Level of enlightenment; are determinants of peace towards nation building. The impact of nations on its populace is not by size, revenue or resources, it is the values placed on citizens as it exists as an entity to make living worthwhile. When adding values to the populace is placed as priority in governance,

it springs reforms that brings forth transformation in sectors that will alleviate values governance crave to see in people, and when the reforms begin to manifest, it automatically maligns the majority from social vices that somewhat affect the stability, and at long run portends as menace.

GOVERNANCE- A MAJOR DRIVE TO NATION BUILDING

A society with no formalized system is no place for normalcy. For a society to attain purpose of creation it must institute an administrative system to govern its affairs in order to achieve its goals and objectives. It is pertinent for emerging nations to first identify and understand the pattern of governance that will be benefitting as this plays a pivotal role for growth and development of any nation.

Governance entails an institutionalized pattern of administration in the political sphere that is subjected to constituted authorities on adequate management of availed resources to effect transformation in the confined territorial landscape and wellbeing of the citizens (Akanni 2022). The term governance can be used specifically to describe changes in the nature and role of the state following the public-sector reforms of the 1980s and 90s. Typically, these reforms are said to have led to a shift from a hierarchic bureaucracy toward a greater use of markets, quasi-markets, and networks, especially in the delivery of public services. Governance, expresses a widespread belief that the state increasingly depends on other organizations to secure its intentions, deliver its policies, and establish a pattern of rule.

Governance is the action of governing an organization by using and regulating influence to direct and control the actions and affairs of management and others. It is the exclusive responsibility of the 'governing body', the person, or group accountable for the performance and conformance of the organization. So virtually, governance is an embodiment of administrative knowledge in applicable to a vast territorial landscape with composition of the citizens and the resources. The governance framework is there to encourage the efficient use of resources and equally to require accountability for the stewardship of those resources. The aim is to align as nearly as possible the interests of individuals, the organization and society.

This is achieved through the design, implementation and ensuring compliance with the five functions of governance. These are:

1. **Determining the objectives of the organization**: expressed through its vision and mission statements and implementation through its strategic plan. The objectives define the purpose of the organization, and describe how the purpose will be fulfilled.
2. **Determining the ethics of the organization:** defining what aspects of behavior are really

important. How much importance is genuinely given to factors such a sustainability, corporate social responsibility and stakeholder engagement over profits and short-term movements in the share process. Ethics are based on morals and values and define the rules or standards governing the conduct of people within the organization.

3. **Creating the culture of the organization:** is a more subtle process and deals with the way people interact with each other. The governing body decides on the culture it wants and influences the operating culture of the organization through the people it appoints to execute positions.

    'Governmentality', the willingness of people to 'be governed' and to support the governance system is at the centre of an effective culture. Other aspects include: how supportive the organization is, how innovative, how risk seeking/averse, how open and transparent, how mature and professional, and how tolerant it is. It is impossible to have a culture of innovation and sensible risk taking if the organization is intolerant of failure.

4. **Ensuring compliance by the organization:** with its regulatory, statutory and legal obligations, as well as ensuring its management and staff work towards achieving the organization's objectives, while working within the ethical and cultural framework defined by the governing body.
5. **Designing and implementing the governance framework for the organization:** The governing body is accountable for the performance of the organization, and retains overall responsibility for the organization it governs; however, in most organizations the governing body cannot undertake all of the work of governance itself.

To ensure the efficient governance of the organization, various responsibilities need to be delegated to people within the organization's management. The governance framework defines the principles, structures, enabling factors and interface through which the organization's governance arrangements will operate by delegating appropriate levels of authority and responsibility to managers and other entities, and ensuring accountability.

In summary, the governing body appoints, provides direction to and oversees the functioning of the organization's management and makes the 'rules' the organization's management and staff are expected to conform to. Working within its ethical and cultural framework, while complying with the 'rules' and providing assurance back to the governing body that this is being accomplished.

The governance system and the management system are symbiotic, but although mutually interdependent, the two systems fulfil very different functions. A well-governed organization is designed to allow these two systems to work together to the benefit of the organization's overall stakeholder community.

This general use of governance enables theorists to explore abstract analyses of the construction of social orders, social coordination, or social practices irrespective of their specific context. Such analyses could be drawn from specific questions about, the state, the international system, or the corporation. However, this general usage creates the need for a more specific term, such as new governance, to refer to the changes in the state since the 1980s. Whether one focuses on the new governance, weak states, or patterns of rule in general, the concept of governance raises issues about public policy and democracy. The increased role of non-state actors in the delivery of public services has led to a concern to improve the ability of the state to oversee these other actors. The state has become more interested in various strategies for creating and managing networks and partnerships. It has set up all kind of arrangement for auditing and regulating other organizations. In addition, the increased role of nonelected actors in policy making suggests need to think about the extent of their democratic accountability and about the mechanisms by which it is enforced.

Governance beyond the State

The literature on new governance highlights the pattern of rule in civil society. The most discussed of these is corporate governance, which is the means of directing and controlling business corporations. The interest in corporate governance is linked to theoretical questions in microeconomics about how to account for stability of firms. Most responses to these questions parallel those that Rational Choice theorists give to questions about the origins of social norms, laws, and institutions. Yet the main source of interest in corporate governance is probably public, shareholder, and governmental concerns about corporate scandals, corruption, abuse of monopoly power, and the high salaries paid to top executives. Three broad themes dominate the resulting literature of corporate ethics. They are openness through disclosure of information, integrity through straightforward dealing, and accountability through a clear division of responsibilities.

Theories of Governance

It is important to recognize that the meaning of governance varies according to not only the level of generality at which it is pitched but also the theoretical contexts in which it is used.

Rational Choice

The neoliberal narrative of governance overlaps somewhat with rational choice theory. Both of them draw on microeconomic analysis, with its attempt to unpack social life in terms of individual actions and to explain individual actions in terms of rationality, and especially profit or utility maximization. Yet, although neoliberals deployed such analysis to promote marketization and the new public management, rational choice theorists were often more interested in exploring cases where institutions or norms where honored even in the absence of a higher authority to enforce them. Rational choice theory attempts to explain all social phenomena by reference to the micro level of rational individual activity. It unpacks social facts, institutions, and patterns of rule entirely by analysis of individual acting. It models individual acting on the assumption that they adopt the course of action most in accord with their preferences to be rational: preferences are assumed to be complete and transitive. At other times, however, rational choice theorists try to relax these unrealistic assumptions by developing concepts of bounded rationality. They then attempt to model human behavior in circumstances where people lack relevant information.

The dominance of the micro level in rational choice theory raises issues about the origins, persistence, and institutions by which people are governed. One issue is the abstract one of how to explain the rise and stability of a pattern of rule in the absence of any higher authority. Rational choice theorists generally conclude that the absence of any effective higher authority means that such institutions have to be conceived as self-enforcing. Another issue is a more specific interest in the effects of norms, laws, and institutions on individuals' action. Rational choice theorists argue that institutions structure people's strategic interactions with one another; stable institutions influence individuals' actions by giving them reasonable expectations about the outcome of the varied courses of action from which they might choose. Another, more specific issue is in models of weakly institutionalized environments in which the absence of a higher authority leads people to break agreements and so create instability. Examples of such weak institutions include the international system and nation states in which the rule of law is weak. Rational Choice theorists explore self-enforcing agreements, the costs associated with them, and the circumstances in which they break down.

The new institutionalism

An institutional approach dominated the study of the state, government, public administration, and politics until about the 1940s. scholars focused on formal rules, procedures, and organizations, including constitutions, electoral systems, and political parties. Although they sometimes emphasized the formal rules that governed such institutions, they also paid attention to the behavior of actors within them. This institutional approach was challenged in the latter half of the 20th century by a series of attempts to craft universal theories: behaviorists, rational choice theorists, and others attempted to explain social action with relatively little reference to specific institutional settings. The new institutionalists retain a focus on rules, procedures, and organizations: institutions are composed of two or more people, they serve some kind of social purpose, and they exist over time in a way that transcends the intentions and actions of specific individuals. But the new institutionalists adopt a broader concept of institution that includes norms, habits, and cultural customs alongside formal rules, procedures, and organizations. It has become common to distinguish various species of new institutionalism. Rational choice institutionalists examine how institutions shape the behavior of rational actors by creating expectations about the likely consequences of given courses of action. They offer two main accounts of how institutions shape behavior. Historical institutionalists tend to use metaphors such as path dependency and to emphasize the importance of macro-level studies of institutions over time. Sociological institutionalists tend to argue that cognitive and symbolic scheme give people identifies and roles. Historical institutionalists focus on the way past institutional arrangements shape responses to political pressures. They argue that past outcomes, having become embedded in national institutions, prompt social groups to organize along particular lines and thereby lock states into paths of development. Hence, they concentrate on comparative studies of welfare and administrative reform across states in which the variety of such reforms is explicable by path dependency. Sociological institutionalists focus on values, identities, and the ways in which these shape actors' perceptions of their interests. They argue that informal sets of ideas and values constitute policy paradigms that shape the ways in which organizations think about issues and conceive of political pressures. They concentrate on studies of the ways in which norms and values shape what are often competing policy agendas of welfare and administrative reform.

Systems theory

Although sociological institutionalism can resemble interpretive theories, it often exhibits a distinctive debt to organizational theory. At times its exponents conceive of cognitive and symbolic schemes not as intersubjective understandings but as properties of organizations. Instead of reducing such schemes to relevant actors, they conceive of them as a kind of system based on its own logic. In doing so, they echo themes that are developed more fully in systems theory. A system is the pattern of order that arises from the regular interactions of a series of interdependent elements. Systems theorists suggest that such patterns of order arise from the functional relations between, and interactions of, the elements. These relations and interactions involve a transfer of information. This transfer of information leads to the self-production and self-organization of the system even in the absence of any centre of control.

The conception of governance highlights the limits of governing by the state. It implies that they are no single sovereign authority. Instead, there is a self-organizing system composed of interdependent actors and institutions. Systems theories often distinguish here between governing, which is goal-directed interventions, and governance, which is the total effect of governing interventions and interactions. In this view, governance is a self-organizing system that emerges from the activities and exchange of actors and institutions. Again, the new governance arose out of the belief that society has become centerless, or at least endowed with multiple centres. From this perspective, order arises from the interactions of multiple centres or organizations. The role of the state is not to create order but to facilitate sociopolitical interactions, to encourage varied arrangements for coping with problems, and to distribute services among numerous organizations.

Regulatory Theory

Just as sociological institutionalism sometimes draws on systems theory, so historical institutionalism sometimes draws on Marxist state theory. The main approach derived from Marxism is, however, regulation theory. Karl Marx argued that capitalism is unstable because it leads to capital overaccumulation and class struggle.

Regulation theories examine the ways in which different varieties of capitalism attempt to manage these instabilities. Their study form of governance in relation to changes in the way these instabilities are masked.

According to regulation theorists, intensive accumulation and monopolistic regulation temporarily created a virtuous circle: mass production created economies of scale, thereby leading to a rise in productivity; increased productivity led to increased wages and so greater consumer demand; the growth in demand meant greater profits because of the full utilization of capacity.

Interpretive theories

Interpretive approach to governance often emphasizes on contingency. They reject the idea that patterns of rule can be properly understood in terms of historical or social logic attached to capitalist development, functional differentiation, or even institutional settings. Instead, they emphasize the meaningful character of human actions and practices. In this view, because people act on beliefs, ideas, or meanings- whether conscious or not- their actions can be explained properly only if the relevant meanings are grasped. The approach suggested that beliefs, ideas, or meanings are more or less uniform across a culture or society. Hence, they inspire studies of the distinctive patterns of governance associated with various cultures. Other interpretive approaches place a greater emphasis on the contents and struggles over meaning that they take to constitute so much political activity.

Although interpretive theorists analyze governance in terms of meanings. The meanings of interest to them are variously described, for example, as intentions and beliefs, conscious or tacit knowledge, subconscious or unconscious assumptions, systems of signs and languages, and discourses and ideologies. Interpretive theorists often explore many of these varied types of meanings both synchronically and diachronically. Synchronic studies analyze the relationship between a set of meanings abstracted from the flux of history. They reveal the internal coherence or pattern of a web of meanings; they make sense of a particular belief, concept, or sign by showing how it fits in such a web. Diachronic studies analyze the development of webs of meaning over time. They show how situated agents modify and even transform webs of meaning as they use them in particular settings.

The diverse interpretive studies of synchronic and diachronic dimensions of meaning all have in common a reluctance to reduce meanings to allegedly objective facts about institutions, systems, or capitalism. In this view, patterns of rule arise because of the contingent triumph of a web of meanings. Sometimes, interpretive studies relate the rise of neoliberalism and network theory to new relations of power, changes in the global economy, or problems confronted by states. Even when they do, however, they usually suggest that these social facts are also constructed in the context of webs of meaning.

The theories of governance clarify the behaviors of people to be the centerpiece of principles that promote public management. As it is that the state is encircled with it affairs on the people, so does the people a determinant to institutions that presides over the formation and structure of organization that oversee on the polity and aid strategic interactions through perceived values and identities which influences the political paradigms to be effective in meeting the expectation of governance. From this, it can now be succinctly said, that **Governance** is managing effectively and subsequently the resources and manpower by the leading elites for the upliftment of the constituent, (Akanni 2020). Mans' decides what society becomes through the selection of procedures of managing affairs in attempt to effectively synchronize with the environment of sustainability; in order to achieve this, administrative pattern is selected to appropriate conducts and activities amongst each other for the development of the environment and the people. In any pattern deem fit chosen, the administrative executive is selected in its own form to pioneer affairs with each member of the leading elites handed with portfolios regarded as expectation from various positions. In respective positions, they are expected to function in line prescribed by conduct of the office during execution of roles in lieu to meeting people's demands and needs. Globally, it's been that successful and developed nations are the ones that have consistently designated administrative style of governance befitting values, cultures and identities against system of governance imposed on nations that apparently take durable period to understand and adapt to for it to work; cases have had it clear that countries noted to have fallen with the categories of struggling nations are the ones that have numerously practiced two or more administrative system of governance, deviating from the initial system it adopted at independent, making shortfalls in governance to understand the system consecutively. System of governance is determinant to countries development and it varies amidst developed nations; base on acceptance by the larger populace and commitment by the leading elites in attaining relevance. It is pertinent to indicate that no system of governance is devoid of effectiveness, as what count most in any system of governance is the enlightenment and orientation of every component of the organization setting; which makes everyone informed on governance pursuit. The administrative pattern across globe certainly differs, and in attempt to properly comprehend the pattern that have somewhat contributed most to developed nations with cogent reasons, it is imperative to identify and examine various administrative pattern.

(1.) **Democratic System:** This is an exercise of governance with a practice of distribution of authorities at various stages of political positions, elected and non-elected. Position of authorities follows a process of selection called "electoral process" where the nationalist clinches tent to preferred candidates. Democracy, as a system of government; literally mean rule by the people. The term is derived from Greek demokratia, which was coined from demo("people") and Kratos("rule") in the middle of the 5th century BCE to denote the political systems then existing in some Greek city-states, notably Athens. Studies of contemporary nonliterate tribal societies and other evidence suggest that democracy, broadly speaking, was practiced within tribes of hunter-gatherers in prehistoric times. The transition to settled agricultural communities led to inequalities of wealth and power between and within communities and hierarchical nondemocratic forms of social organization. Thousands of years later, in the 6th century BCE, a relatively democratic form of government was introduced in the city-state of Athens by Cleisthenes.

To properly comprehend the formation of this principle of governance, it is needful to have insight on propounded theories of the system.

Theories of Democracy

Pericles

In a funeral oration in 430 BCE for those who had fallen in the Peloponnesian War, the Athenian leader Pericles described democratic Athens as "the school of Hellas." Among the city's many exemplary qualities, he declared, which "favors the many instead of the few; this is why it is called democracy." Pericles continued: "If we look to the laws, they afford equal justice to all in their private differences; if to social standing, advancement in public life falls to reputation for capacity, class considerations not being allowed to interfere with merit; nor again does poverty bar the way; if a man is able to serve the state, he is not hindered by obscurity of his condition. The freedom which we enjoy in our government extends also to our ordinary life.

Aristotle

A century later, Aristotle discussed democracy in terms of that that would become highly influential in comparative studies of political systems. At the heart of his approach is the notion of a "constitution," which he defines as "an organization of offices, which all the citizens distribute among themselves, according to power which different classes possess." He concludes that "there must therefore be as many forms of government as there are modes of arranging the offices, according to the superiorities and the differences of the parts of the state." Even the realist, however, he remarks that "the best [government] is often unattainable, and therefore the true legislator and statesman ought to be acquainted, not only with (1) that which is best in the abstract, but also with (2) that which is best relatively to circumstances.

Aristotle identifies three kinds of ideal constitution- each of which describes a situation in which those who rule pursue the common good-and the corresponding kinds of perverted constitution-each of which describes a situation in which those who rule pursue narrow and selfish goals. The three kinds of constitution, both ideal and perverted, are differentiated by the number of persons they allow to rule. Thus, "rule by one" is monarchy in its ideal form and tyranny in its perverted form; "rule by the few" is aristocracy in its ideal form and oligarchy in its perverted form; and "rule by the many" is "polity" in its ideal form and democracy in its perverted form.

Aristotle took a more favorable view of democracy in his studies of the variety, stability, and composition of actual democratic governments. In his observation that "the basis of a democratic state is liberty," Aristotle proposed a connection between the ideas of democracy and liberty that would be strongly emphasized by all later advocates of democracy.

John Locke

Nearly 20 centuries after Aristotle, the English philosopher John Locke adopted the essential elements of the Aristotelian classification of constitutions in his Second Treatise of Civil Government (1690). Unlike Aristotle, however, Locke was an unequivocal supporter of political equality, individual liberty, democracy, and majority rule. Although his work was naturally rather abstract and not particularly programmatic, it provided a powerful philosophical foundation for much later democratic theorizing and political programs.

The legitimacy of government

According to Locke, in the hypothetical "state of nature" that precedes the creation of human societies, men live "equal one amongst another without subordination or subjection," and they are perfectly free to act and to dispose of their possessions as they see fit, within the bounds of natural law. From these and other premises Locke draws the conclusion that political society-i.e.., government- insofar as it is legitimate, represents a social contract among those who have "consented to make one community or Government ... wherein the Majority have a right to act and conclude the rest." These two ideas- the consent of the governed and majority rule- became central to all subsequent theories of democracy. For Locke they are inextricably connected: "For if the consent of the majority shall not in reason, be received, as the act of the whole, and conclude every individual; nothing but the consent of every individual can make anything be the act of the whole: but such a consent is next to impossible ever to be had." Thus, no government is legitimate unless it enjoys the consent of the governed, and that consent cannot be rendered except through majority rule.

Locke's description of the different forms of government (which he regarded as the "commonwealth") does not explicitly prescribe democracy as the only legitimate system. The passages of the Second Treatise show that Locke remains true to his fundamental principle, that the only legitimate form of government is that based on the consent of the governed. Locke differentiates the various forms of government on the basis of where the people choose to place the power to make laws. His categories are the traditional ones: If the people retain the legislative power for themselves, together with the power to appoint those who execute the laws, then "the form of government is a perfect democracy." If they put the power "into the hands of a few select Men, and their Heirs or Successors, then it is an Oligarchy: Or else into the hands of one Man, and then it is a Monarchy." For whatever the form of government, the ultimate source of sovereign power is the people, and all legitimate government must rest on their consent.

Montesquiue

The French political theorist Montesquiue, through his masterpiece The Spirit of the Laws (1748). Montesquiue distinguishes three ideal types of government: monarchy, "in which a single person governs by fixed and established laws"; despotism, "in which a single person directs everything by his own will and caprice"; and republican government, which may be of two types, depending on whether "the body, or only a part of the people, is possessed of the supreme power," the former being a democracy, the latter an aristocracy.

According to him, a necessary condition for the existence of a republican government, whether democratic or aristocratic, is that the people in whom supreme power is lodged possess the quality of "public virtue," meaning that they are motivated by a desire to achieve the public good. Although public virtue may not be necessary in a monarchy and is certainly absent in despotic regimes, it must be present to some degree in aristocratic republics and to a large degree in democratic republics. He asserted that without strong public virtue, a democratic republic is likely to be destroyed by conflict between various "factions," each pursuing its own narrow interests at the expense of a broader public good.

Ironically, the democratic dispensation is not limited to the system of governance. A democratic society is that with regards to the people and the rule of law irrespective of the pattern of governance being practiced. Till the 21st century, the alignment of the democratic and parliamentary pattern has been largely misconstrued to the democratic system of governance even though they share the peculiarity of conducting election for decisive leaders. As I process, considerations shall be provided to differentiate and examine both respective roles in the polity.

From the narrative, a democratic system is where the rule of law as stipulated by the constitution are adhere to by the components of a nation; and a democratic system comprises four arms of governance: (i) The Executive "constitute authority to oversee the administrative affairs of governance," (ii) Legislative "is regarded as the constitutional chamber representing the people and responsible for the nations' constitutional formation," (iii) Judiciary "regard the constitution as outlined documents binding the activities of the nation and also responsible for interpretation of constitution as the law of the territorial landscape," (iv) Citizens "whom supreme power is lodged due to the quality of public virtue it possesses."

(1) **Democratic/Presidential-** The executive position in the democratic system entails the presidential and gubernatorial positions which passes through series of electoral policies designed primarily for selective purpose. In order to be selected as the president/governor the candidates must initially win the nomination of a major political party before competing against rival candidates in other political parties at the federation election

which all eligible citizens of the country possess the civil responsibilities to vote and be voted for. In this scenario, the candidates with the highest quarter/points of votes casted is recognized by the constitution as the winner of electoral process that is coordinated by the electoral body. It is a pattern that operate with periodicals; mostly covering a span of four years tenures with a possible chance of re-election of additional term. The executives, by the constitution are recognized with authorities to exercise administrative affairs towards national development of the nation state, and the position is regarded as the utmost seat in polity as it is tagged the Head of state of a republican nation.

(i) **The legislatives**- The essence of democracy is for the will of the people to triumph; this arm is regarded as the constitutional chamber representing the people and responsible for the nations' constitutional formation. Legislature is an assembly with the authority to make laws for a political entity. The legislative branch consists of the House of Representatives and the Senate. The constitution grants the arm the sole authority to enact legislation, the right to confirm or reject many presidential appointments, establishing the government's budget, ratifying treaties, redressing constituents' grievances, impeaching and removing from office members of the executive and judiciary, and substantial investigative power. Members of the House are elected with specific duration stipulated by the constitution to represent their constitutes. Public policy making is their priority, as this is what is interpreted into responsive action that effect national development that in turn impact the public space.

(ii) **Judiciary**- the judiciary is the system of courts that interprets, defends, and applies the law in the name of the state. The judiciary can also be thought of as the mechanism for the resolution of disputes. Under the doctrine of separation of powers, the judiciary generally does not make statutory law (which is the responsibility of the legislature) or enforce law (which is the responsibility of the executive), but rather interprets, defends, and applies the law to the facts of each case.

In many jurisdictions the judicial branch has the power to change laws through the process of judicial review. Courts with judicial review power may annul the laws and rules of the state when it finds them incompatible with a higher norm, such as primary legislation, the provisions of the constitution, treaties or international law. Judges constitute a critical force for interpretation and implementation of a constitution.

(iii) **Citizens**- "whom supreme power is lodged due to the quality of public virtue it possesses." There is no state sovereignty that has legitimacy in itself. The famous three opening words of the United States constitution; 'We the people...,' express this principle: the constitution derives its power from the people. **Citizenship** can be defined as the total of all the right and principle accorded to all members of a given state. Member of any state carries with it some right, duties and obligations of its members who are then referred to as citizens. It is a responsibility in the public domain that can be referred to as citizenship as office.

OBLIGATIONS OF CITIZENS

(a) Prompt payment of taxes.
(b) Obedience to the law of the state.
(c) Defense of the state against internal and external enemies.
(d) Upholding the honor and dignity of the state.
(e) Paying supreme sacrifice for the state when the need arises

RIGHTS OF CITIZENS

(a) Freedom of Worship/religion
(b) Freedom of movement
(c) Right to life
(d) Right to private and family
(e) Right to association
(f) Right to vote and be voted for
(g) Right to own moveable and immovable property anywhere
(h) Freedom of expression and the press.

The democratic system is financial intensive to operate as the electoral process requires substantial funds consecutively to conduct elections subsequently. It is apparently the most expensive system to operate; with the nature of autonomy for the three tiers of governance, at the federal, state, and local level, the system is imbibed with financial authorities on overall expenditures. The peculiarity of repetition of likened electoral positions due to creation of modular territories or states, carts large portion of accrued revenue earmarked for recurrent expenditures; leaving a flimsy portion for capital expenditures. For developing nations, the system is a pest on utility of revenue and resources as only the few leading elites within the category of governance benefit more from the coffers than the majority, resulting to decay of amenities and lack of basic infrastructures.

(2.) **Parliamentary/Prime Minister**- It is the other side of coin of the democratic system and one of the oldest in practice of governance. This pattern only accommodates electoral process for the legislative arm; and the dominant parties representing at the federal/regional legislative chambers decides and select who and what constitute the executive council. The electoral seat in the legislative chamber serves as electoral point of the constituents allotted to it representative whom it is empowered by the electoral act to be applied during electoral procedure of the Prime Minister. At the floor of the chamber, the decisive winner is regarded as the Prime Minister who oversee activities and assumed the position of Head of government/state. It operates on periodicals; with a span of five years tenure and a possible chance of re-election of additional term. It is a self-determination style of governance comprising a confederating unit of people with similarities, interest, beliefs and values; with each group represented at the legislative chambers. The benefit is the synergy it adopts on elective positions and roles into a singular unit. This pattern enables moderate overall expenditures and sizable recurrent expenditures; and avails appropriate utility of accrued revenue and resources on capital expenditures. Like the democratic system, the parliamentary system comprises four arms of governance: (i) The Executive/Prime Minister "constitute authority to oversee the administrative affairs of governance," (ii) Legislative "is regarded as the constitutional chamber representing the people and responsible for the nations' constitutional formation," (iii) Judiciary "regard the constitution as outlined documents binding the activities of the nation and also responsible for interpretation of constitution as the law of the territorial landscape," (iv) Citizens "whom supreme power is lodged due to the quality of public virtue it possesses."

(3.) **Monarchy System-** It is the traditional parliamentary system from time immemorial that birthed the modern parliamentary style of governance. It maintains a sizeable cabinet that can be regarded as the legislative, and members known as chiefs. The Head of Government/State and of the leading elites is a "Crown King." Every position follows a process of selection ascribed by the tradition. The chiefs are advisory and serve as body that check and balances activities of the king. It is virtually the system that led to modern day polity and its impact and practice is felt among nations that still absorb it as a pattern of governance. Because of the size of the cabinet, the overall expenditure incurred is minimal, availing the authorities' sufficient revenue and resources for capital expenditures. This system has brought significant growth and development to nations such as the Kingdom of Saudi Arabia, UAE, and some North African countries.

(4.) **Imperialism**- At all point of human existence, civility come to play. Imperialism is the combination of monarchy and parliamentary system of governance with recognition of the Throne as the Head of State. It antecedent is dated back to 1653 in the British commonwealth after dissolution of the initial 1649 Parliamentary Act took effect, afterwards, the Army Council adopted the instrument of Government which made a united Commonwealth of England, Wales, Scotland and Ireland. Due to Oliver Cromwell death as the Lord Protector of the United Commonwealth in 1659; the protectorate parliament was dissolved, recalled and started the process that led to restoration of the monarchy in 1660 and recognition of the throne as Head of State. The dissolution of the instrument of government that acknowledged the Lord protectorate as the Head of State of the British Commonwealth was amended and reconstituted to recognition of the Throne as Head of State and still acknowledges the constitutional roles of the parliament as Head of government with the role of the Prime Minister as Head of the parliamentary system. The Prime Ministers' appointment is however subjected to recognition by the Throne with which is vested authority to acknowledge or disprove the appointments of Prime Minister.

(5.) **Militarization system**- It is an exercise of authority by the defense council coordinating political and administrative affairs of its territory. The most senior military officers assume positions of authority with designated roles of respective administrative ranks. And the activities of the administrators are checked by the military council that performs the legislative roles. The head of this pattern of governance is regarded as the military head of state and exercises authority that vetoes decisions. The effectiveness of the military administrator is actually base on personal attribute of leadership in most situations. This is a system of governance peculiar to the African continent, and that has marred its growth and development due to years of misrule and mismanagement. It has truncated the establishment of some political terrain caused by immaturity of the political elites resulting to political instability and crisis within its fold. The only country that had a prolonged practice of this system with substantial growth was Libya during the Late Muhamal Gadaffi regime as head of affairs of the country for several years, which was halted by political phenomena that swept most Arab countries in 2011, tagged "the Arab uprising" a form of agitation clamoring for change of leadership/governances. The uprising eventually led to civil war, destroying decades of accomplishments, and altering the political landscape and stability of the country.

In the polity, we often misconstrued the executive roles as being responsible for nation building; while their roles are significant to national development; it is not limited to the authority at which governance is fully effected. The question we should often ask are the factors that hinders nation building, and also a considerate insight to nations that have been relatively affected by conflict/revolution which in turn alters the political establishment. Let's not forget to be reminded, that the affairs of nations are duly guided by the legislative arm whose responsibilities are to outlines policies from their experience of democratic system, collective memory formation, economic reconstruction, and peacebuilding process.

Expression to dissatisfaction are common phenomena in the political space, and what a proactive polity can do is to enhance the policy makers to establish the framework that curtails the displeasure to avoid being denigrated to conflicts or revolution as historically linked to the French revolution which took place in 1789 and ended in late 1790s. During this period the French citizens radically altered the political landscape by uprooting centuries-old institutions of the monarchy and the feudal system which was caused by disgust with the French aristocracy and the economic policies. The French Revolution helped to shape modern democracies by showing the power inherent in the will of the people. Making France the first to embrace democracy as a nation from imperialism.

Disgust interpret lapses in policies that potentially could lead to political revolution if not properly handled by the legislative and executive arm to address the concerns of the people. This, from indication as an entity that functions on its own terms needs to adopt means of normalizing the abnormalities as perceived by the citizens to redress the issue of displeasure; and this can

only be made possible by enacting public policies that are people centric towards nation building.

PUBLIC POLICY AND NATION BUILDING

As earlier stated, the skepticism of peace is war, and wars does not evolve without internal revolt against external pressure. Since territorial landscape are human establishment of occupied entities, and with innate desires for more territorial dominance; the tendency of conflicts will always be visible in human existence with the desires to expand the capacity of one's control. The formation of nations is basis on territorial establishment. Prior to a nation attainment of an independent state, the collective will of the people must prevail by first identifying to the nation state with a common purpose of togetherness towards national development that is primarily aimed at building a nation. As we gradually proceed in modernization, hence, its yields of civility for a more organized society. The wars that evolves in the 16th and 17th centuries led to the adoption of Westphalain peace treaties of 1648 to reconciles conflicts with warring parties and to present a definite ground establishment for both parties by which the rifts are settled and also eliminating reoccurrence of the event. The westphalain peace treaties created the platform for policies enactment for the recognition of nations that pave ways for diplomacy in the global scene and balancing bilateral activities between nations.

In the process of establishing an egalitarian and equity atmosphere in the society, a nation must place its ethical conducts as utmost priority in realization of its potential. National development is a process of fundamental merits in enactment of policies that aids nation building. In building a nation, the ideologies and policies must be structure for the wellbeing of the citizen and in manner that it continually evolves with new trends in the ecosystem.

Nation-building is a significant undertaking that government employ to develop political, economic, security, and social institutions which determines the progressiveness of a country. In whatever aspect the policies are formed, it is towards the betterment of the public; so, the principles of public policies lay on the will of the people to benefit from the dividends of governance. And since governance is a decisive process of implementation of public services, which basically has to do with addressing public necessities that are vital for the wellbeing of the people; the procedure at which these services are rendered by appropriate authorities is what is regarded as "Public Policy."

Essentially, public policy is a set of laws, guidelines, and actions decided and taken by governments in order to work in favor of the public. Public policy can dictate things such as: which laws are passed, where funding goes, and which topics concern the general public. Often, policies are debated and negotiated between parties and different interests, and can also involve parties that are not in government, such as experts in fields of professional disciplines. In general, public policies are shaped over a number of years and there are several institutions that will contribute to the formation and details of a specific policy. Public policies are there to influence how other important decisions are made, and it's usually formed as responses to specific issues that are of interest to the public. The formulation of policies is regarded as major aspect in nations affairs that propels countries functionalities and serve as scale that measures and determines national development. The established policies are pattern by which all activities are to be conducted and regulated by respective agencies whom it's been aligned to perform it roles on behalf of the government. Policies formulation is not only streamline to the government alone, it is a combination of Public and Private Partnership of professionals in diverse disciplines to outline ethical conducts during implementation of public services. These combinations of professionals are what is regarded as 'Policy makers.'

Examples of social problems that government makes and implement policies to solve includes, unemployment, insecurity, poor standard in education, dwindling national income, corruption, low quantity in agricultural production, inflation, low standard of industrial products, poor health system, poor access to financial services for economic activities, rising social and economic inequality, political, religious, social and ethnic violence or agitation, poor transportation system, poor housing system, drug abuse, rape and poor public service delivery.

Characteristic of Public Policy

- It outlines the pattern of solving a particular problem.
- It is goal oriented. In essence, policy is directed at attainment of certain goals or objectives.
- It is a response by the political system to challenges and problems arising from the environment.
- It is usually designed to effect a given target population in a defined geographical entity.
- It is a process that runs through formulation to implementation and to evaluation and through feedback; may result to modification of an existing policy or formulation of a different policy considered to be more appropriate.

- It is generally the potent instrument for the pursuit of development.

Types of Public Policy Making Models

- **Rational comprehension model:** On the basis of this model, public policy is arrived at by considering all alternatives and their consequences with aim of arriving at a more appropriate policy option. The rational comprehension model has the merit of being thorough and scientific in approach to arriving at a policy option.
- **Incremental model:** This model emphasizes small or incremental addition or modification in an already existing policies as a solution to problems or challenges. This type of policy is usually conservative.
- **Mixed scanning:** Mixed scanning model entails a process of arriving at a public policy through adopting the features of rational comprehension model and incremental model.
- **The satisfy model:** In use of this model, a public policy is arrived at by choosing the alternative that is satisfactory, good enough and feasible rather than the optimal alternatives

Theories of Public Policy

Theories of public policy making is concerned with the identification and discussion of the source of public policy in terms of who makes or influence the content of public policy, the direction of public policy flow and the interest that public policies serve.

(i) **The system Theory:** this theory states that input in form of demand and support comes from the environment into the political system that process them and bring them out as output in form of goods and services. In essence, according to this system theory, public policies are responses of the political system to the problems, challenges, aspiration which their solutions are made as demands on the political system by the environment. The political system in specific terms that process these demand (inputs) consist of the public institution like the legislative arm of government, the executive arm and the judicial arm.

(ii) **The Elite Theory:** This theory sees the source or the makers of public policies as well as the interests that policies are meant to serve as the elites. This assumption is a consequence of the fact that the elite's theory believes that the society is divided into two – the masses and the elites.

(iii) **The Group Theory:** The group theory of public policy assumes that public policy is the equilibrium or compromise reached in group struggle or competition for favorable allocation or re-allocation of values in the society. This group theory assumes that public policies are usually made in the interest or favor of the most influential groups in the society.

In order to ensure greater influence and more favorable allocation of values, groups all work to enhance their access to the key points of policy making. Usually the level of influence of any group depends on its leadership, resources and strategic position.

Groups in this context refer to social, political, economic, religious, or occupational groups in the society. Groups as source of public policy by this theory is a consequence of the theory assumption that the society is a mosaic of groups and that these groups continue to interact and compete for the authoritarian allocation of values by the political system through policy pronouncement.

(iv) **The Institutional Theory:** This theory assumes that public policy is often initiated, formulated and implemented by government institutions. Consequently, it assumes further that institutional analysis concentrating on structures, procedures and relationship with each other can help in understanding policy formulation and implementation. Using this theory, the focus on policy analysis would be the executive, legislature and judicial bodies or arms of government.

Policy Development

Policy development in polity is the process undertaken by the government to meet needs, protect rights, distribute resources, enforce laws, create laws, amend current laws, provide well-being, protect citizens, and any other national interest topic. The purpose of public policy is to hold lawmakers and representatives accountable in making laws that are essential to the public's wellbeing. Once the lawmakers create a law then it is the responsibility of government workers to enforce these laws or to carry out the policy. Public policy can impact everyday life from minor events to more major or long-term events.

Public officials, government workers, and government organizations work together to produce action in order to take on the challenge of public issues. Policy development can take a long time to prepare, pass as a law, and execute into action. The political system is very fluid meaning officials are often running for election and office holders take critical roles in the policy making process. The first development step usually begins with an issue or a problem that needs to be resolved. Public policy is usually a reactionary event meaning policy is passed in response to public needs or a problem.

Government officials will usually address the issue first and tell the public how it affects them. Then they will let the public know what is being, or will be, done to help fix the issue. At last public officials and public organization will create policy to address the issue and take action to resolve it.

Policy Issue

A policy issue means any topic or category that is a source of problems or conflict in the public. Public policy issues refer to what the government is doing about policy issues. Policy issues can also describe what the government is not doing in related to certain topics.

Policy Making Process

The public policy making process involves 5 main steps following the traditional model: Agenda setting, policy formation, decision making, policy implementation, and policy evaluation.

Problem Identification

The first step in the policy making process is to identify a problem that impacts the public. Problem identification should also have details to the cause of the problem. This step is also part of the agenda setting phase. It is known as the agenda setting phase because the political leadership in power will be the ones responsible with picking the issues that take priority. The issues that resources are distributed too will be weighed upon public interest as well as issues that the public feel like they can support.

Identification of Policy Options

The next phase of the policy process is to develop options to address the issue. This part of the process involves picking reasonable options to solve the problem. There are many alternatives that are identified in this stage. This stage typically consists of debates between parties who want their option to be the main solution to address the issue

Selection and Implementation

Once the options are weighed and the best option is selected, the next phase is implementation of the policy. A cost-benefit analysis is used to weigh the costs and the benefits to see if the implementation will be beneficial. This step puts the chosen option to solve the issue into effect. The government officials use the public policy tolls and public resources to create change and take action towards solving the issue.

The willingness of absolute regulation of all sectors of the countries affairs led to the involvement of the legislative and the executive arm of governance in dictating the pattern of operations in sectors internally, and externally in bilateral relations. It is obvious that the performance of key sectors has direct implications on the peoples' wellbeing and the index performance of governance base on its policies. Every country does have their peculiar policies in ways befitting to entities; the policies on key factors such as political, economic, security, and social institutions are significant to countries index performances and peoples' wellbeing. In furtherance, policies on these factors differs and most likely are a times, as applicable to countries, are interwoven with administrative pattern of governance. Comprehension of the economic policies are pivotal towards nation building, and it's important to understand how it contribute to national development of countries: the three main economic theories which economic policies are formulated from are -

Capitalism Economy

Capitalism or capitalist economy is referred to as the economic system where the factors of production such as capital goods, labor, natural resources, and entrepreneurship is controlled and regulated by private businesses. In a capitalist economy, the production of all the goods and services is dependent on the demand and supply in the market that is also known as a market that is also known as a market economy. It is different from the central planning system that is also known as a command economy or a planned economy. The main characteristic of a capitalist economy is the motive of earning profit. The capitalist economy is also characterized by the presence of free markets and lack of participation by the government in regulating the business.

The origin of capitalism can be traced back to 18th century England that was undergoing the industrial revolution at that time. As there is no government intervention in this type of economy, it is also known as a free market economy.

Features of Capitalism

1. **Private property:** This is one of the most important characteristics of capitalism where private properties like factories, machines, and equipment can be owned by private individuals or companies.
2. **Freedom of enterprise:** Under this system, every individual has the right to make their own economic decisions without any interference. This is applicable to both consumers and producers.
3. **Profit motive:** The motive of earning profit is one of the most important drivers of a capitalist economy. In this system, all the companies are looking to produce and sell their products to consumers to ear maximum profit.
4. **Price mechanism:** Under this system, the demand and supply in the market will determine the production level and correspondingly the price set for the products without any kind of involvement from the government.
5. **Consumer sovereignty:** In this system, the market is controlled by the demands of the consumer. It regulates the level of production undertaken by the companies, and the consumer is free to decide which products to purchase.

6. **Free trade:** In this system, the low tariff barriers exist that promote international trade.
7. **Government interference:** In a capitalist economy, there is no government interference in the daily activities of the business. The customers and producers are free to make their own decisions regarding any product or service.
8. **Flexibility in labor markets:** In capitalism, there is a flexibility in hiring and firing of the workforce.
9. **Freedom of ownership:** In this system, an individual can accumulate any amount of property and use it according to his will. After death, the same property is passed on to successors by the right of inheritance.

Advantages of Capitalist Economy

1. There is more efficiency in the capitalist economy as the products are produced according to the demand of the consumers.
2. There is less intervention from the government or bureaucratic interference.
3. There is better scope for innovation as companies look to obtain a major of the market with their offerings.

4. It discourages any form of discrimination so that the trade can take place between two parties without any barriers.

Disadvantages of Capitalism Economy

1. Capitalism leads to inequalities in income.
2. In capitalism, firms can get monopoly over workers and consumers.
3. A high profit-earning motive of a capitalist economy is to use resources in such a way that it leads to environmental problems by destroying the natural balance.

Socialist Economy

In the 1840s a new type of economic theory emerged in the literary circles known as "The Communist Manifesto". Written by Karl Marx with Fredric Engels, they propounded a new and unique concept of an economy of a country. This came to be known as a socialist economy. In a socialist economy, the composition is exactly opposite to that of a capitalist economy. In such an economy the factors of production are all state-owned. So, all the factories, machinery, plants, capital, etc. is owned by a community in control of the state.

All citizens get the benefits from the production of goods and services on the basis of equal rights. Hence this type of economy is also known as the Command Economy. So basically, in a socialist economy, private companies or individuals are not allowed to freely manufacture the goods and services. And the production occurs according to the needs of the society and at the command of the state or the Planning Authorities. The market and the factors of supply and demand will pay no role here.

The ultimate aim of a socialist economy is to ensure the maximization of wealth of a whole community, a whole country. It aims to have an equal distribution of wealth amongst all its citizens, not just the welfare of its richest companies and individuals.

Features of Socialist Economy

The main features of socialist economy are as follows:

(i) **Collective Ownership:**
In a socialist economy, the entire foundation is based on socio-economic objectives. The welfare of the people takes precedence over the profit motive. And so all major factors and resources of production are in the ownership of the state itself. Only small farms and trading forms are kept under private ownership.

(ii) **Central Economic Planning:**

In a socialist economy, there is always a central planning committee. This is the authority who will decide what is to be produced using the state resources. They will also decide the quantity and the method of production. The ultimate aim of such authority is to fulfill the socio-economic aims of the State.

(iii) **Equal Distribution of Income:**

This is one of the main features of a socialist economy. The composition does not allow one person to accumulate a lot of wealth. So, the gap between the rich and the poor is much narrower. And all their citizens enjoy equal opportunities and facilities like education, public healthcare, etc. so there is no discrimination between different classes of people.

(iv) **Absence of Market Forces:**

The motive here is the welfare of the people. Since there is no profit motive price mechanism will not influence any product decisions. The pricing structure in a socialist economy is 'administered pricing' which is set by the planning commission on the basis of their socio-economic objectives.

Demerits of Socialist Economy

- Socialism is a breeding ground for corruption, and favoritism. The state and the Central Planning Authority hold too much of the power which they often abuse for their personal gains.
- It essentially restricts the freedom of its citizens. They do not have a choice in the products they wish to buy, or the jobs they want to do. Their freedom is further curtailed by the inability to own any private property.
- Every citizen has the guarantee of a job. So, socialism does not promote hard work or any creativity in its citizens.
- Administered prices are not the most efficient. They are not based on market forces. Thus, the economic and scientific allocation of resources is impossible in this system.
- Sometimes under socialism, we end up creating state monopolies which can get very dangerous with time.

Communist Economy

Communism, political and economic doctrine that aims to replace private property and a profit-based economy with public ownership and communal control of at least the major means of production (e.g., mines, mills, and factories) and the natural resources of a society. Communism is thus a form of socialism- a higher and more advance form, according to its advocates. Exactly how communism differs from socialism has long been a matter of debate, but the distinction rests largely on the communists' adherence to the revolutionary socialism of Karl Marx.

Marx tended to use the terms communism and socialism interchangeably. In his Critique of the Gotha Programme (1875), however, Marx identified two phases of the communism that would follow the predicted overthrow of capitalism: the first would be a transitional system in which the working class would control the government and economy, and the second would be fully realized communism- a society without class divisions or government, in which the production and distribution of goods would be based upon the principle "From each according to his ability, to each according to his needs.

The different economic theories are patterns of coordination of the nation's resources which inevitably reflect in the country's social indexes in correlation to the standard of living. Specifically, the socio-economic aspect of the people is yardstick to sustaining a peaceful atmosphere in countries. The adoption of economy theories in lieu to an effective governance is vital in the affluent of nations, as it determines the prompt management of resources and revenue as applied to effect national development. The three economic theories certainly have its features and disadvantages, and an effective governance will not stick his hills on one. The economic sectors of countries are diverse, likewise governance with its primary aim to focus on the people welfare. To avoid deviating from the norm, a sensitive government must place a balance in the economy policies by abstracting the positive components from the economic theories that effectively addresses specific sectors in the economy, to the benefit of the government, the people, and the private sectors. This, when promptly effected, ratifies the inequalities that could emanate from the distribution of wealth amidst the people, and since the society is not a composition of a particularly homogeneous set of people but rather heterogeneous in nature, we should therefore, by all means possible, try to establish a balance scale in policies formulations to minimize the disparity in social stratification.

The concept of **social stratification** narrative the issue of inequality has been a problem for centuries due to stratification. It emphasized on how socially differentiated men are treated as socially unequal from the point of view of enjoyment of social rewards like status, power, income etc. That may be called social inequality. The term social inequality simply refers to the existence of socially created inequalities.

Social stratification is a particular form of social inequality. All societies arrange their members in terms of superiority, inferiority, and equality. Stratification is a process of interaction or differentiation whereby some people come to rank higher than others.

In one word, when individuals and groups are ranked, according to some commonly accepted basis of valuation in a hierarchy of status levels based upon the inequalities of social positions, social stratification occurs. Social stratification means division of society into different strata or layers. It involves a hierarchy of social groups.

Regarding the origin of stratification many views have been give.

(i) According to Davis, social stratification has come into being due to the functional necessity of the social system.

(According to Karl Marx, social factors are responsible for the emergence of different social strata.

- (ii) According to Spengler, social stratification is founded upon scarcity which is created whenever society differentiates positive in terms of functions and powers.
- (iii) Racial differences accompanied by dissimilarity also leads to stratification.

Types of Social Stratification:

The major types of stratification are

- (i) Caste:
  Is a hereditary endogamous social group in which a person's rank and its accompanying rights and obligations are ascribed on the basis of his birth into a particular group.
- (ii) Class:
  Stratification on the basis of dominant in modern society. In this, a person's position depends to a very great extent upon achievement and his ability to use to advantage the inborn characteristics and wealth that he may possess.
- (iii) Estate: This provides another system of stratification which gave much emphasis to birth as well as to wealth and possessions.

The origin of conflicts and revolutions are aligned to disparities that emanated from the origin of social stratification which pinpoint on the facts that:

(a) The willingness to establish a social structure from a dysfunctional social system with diverse ideological attachments.
(b) The attempt for territorial dominance amongst groups in a confined landscape.
(c) Racial differences from cultural and tribal ethnocentrism.
(d) Displeasure to a social structure perceived as dysfunctional social system to civility for the people's wellbeing.

CONFLICTS, REVOLUTION, AND NATION BUILDING

No nations can absolutely eliminate the possibility of conflicts and revolutions. The reality of man outliving laws and policies is certain in the modern world. Laws and policies are not meant to be rigid by nature, and in a structural political system; provisions should be provided in the constant reviewal of constitution to periodically altered significant components in all laws and policies binding the activities of a nation state. Failures of amendment of flaws from existing policies by the political elites could later be perceived as factors of displeasure from public services which ought to have been rectified by governance due to trend on global event on such activities. Displeasure as a case of dissatisfaction are often firstly expressed verbally as opinions to the political elites whom they assumed are in appropriate positions to evaluate the public services in accordance to the policies and to comprehend if the actual causes of displeasure from the public service is constitutional/policies related or manmade mostly from agencies/official whose responsibility it is to have the public service under control before escalating to a national phenomenon.

A neglected public service, is a time bomb waiting to explode especially if it affects the nationhood. Conflicts and revolutions in any nation, emanates from public services; and before I take a dive on what they are, it's impacts, and how it's affected nation states; it is imperative to have a comprehension of what public services is.

Public Issues

Public issues are situations that affect all people or part of the population in a certain place. They can be of economic, social, cultural or environmental nature and might arise within a city, state, country or globally. As a citizen of a country and a member of a community, there might be times when we feel affected by different problems in domains of public services that are supposed to be of beneficial to the people; understanding public issues might seem complex. There are different parties and interests involved and information often comes from very different sources. Public issues are societal problems that are collectively encountered by the people from the services provided by the government and agencies attached; and if not propelling addressed by a proactive governance that conceives and analyzes the problem and simultaneously take measures on resolution of the problem to avoid it escalation and eliminate the flaws in public services to restore and bestow the integrity of the government on the people through restoration of the public service.

Many conflicts, uprisings and revolutions have emanated from neglected public issues aggravated through years of discord and accumulated grievances by the people towards the government in its failure to rectified social problems that the people have longed proclaimed to the authorities. Any unrest caused by the ineffectiveness of the government is a product of the government, so is the case of the first revolution in the world 'the French Revolution, the 'Arab Uprising', and so many conflicts that have took place afterwards. So, for us to understand the importance of attaching meaning to the people yelling's, the government needs to have a view of what revolution means to have a clarity on the purpose of governance and the roles it need plays in the public domain for the beneficiary of the people in order to sustain a peaceful atmosphere in its entity.

FRENCH REVOLUTION

Bonaparte. During this period, French citizens radically altered their political landscape, uprooting centuries-old institutions such as the monarchy and the feudal system.

The upheaval was caused by disgust with the French aristocracy and the economic policies of King Louis XVI, who met his death by guillotine, as did his wife Marie

Antoinette. Though it degenerated into a bloodbath during the Reign of Terror, the French Revolution helped to shape modern democracies by showing the power inherent in the will of the people.

Causes of the French Revolution

As the 18th century drew to a close, France's costly involvement in the American Revolution, combined with extravagant spending by the king Louis XVI, had left France on the brink of bankruptcy. Not only were the royal coffers depleted, but several years of poor harvests, drought, cattle disease and skyrocketing bread prices had kindled unrest among peasants and the urban poor. Many expressed their desperation and resentment towards a regime that imposed heavy taxes- yet failed to provide any relief -by rioting, looting and striking.

In the fall of 1786, Louis XVI's controller general, Charles Alexandre reform package that included a universal land tax from which the aristocratic classes would no longer be exempt.

Estates General

To garner support for these measures and forestall a growing aristocratic revolt, the king summoned the Estates General- an assembly representing France's clergy, nobility and middle class – for the first time since

1614. The meeting was scheduled for May 5, 1789; in the meantime, delegates of the three estates from each locality would compile lists of grievances to present to the king.

Rise of the Third Estate

France's population, of course, had changed considerably since 1614. The non-aristocratic, middle class members of the Third Estate now represented 98 percent of the people but could still be outvoted by the other two bodies. In the lead-up to the May 5 meeting, the third Estate began to mobilize support for equal representation and the abolishment of the noble veto- in other words, they wanted voting by head and not by status. While all of the orders shared a common desire for fiscal and judicial reform as well as a more representative form of government, the nobles in particular were loath to give up the privileges they had long enjoyed under the traditional system.

Tennis Court Oath

By the time the Estates General convened at Versailles, the highly public debate over its voting process had erupted into open hostility between the three orders, eclipsing the original purpose of the meeting and the authority of the man who had convened it – the king himself. On June 17, with talks over procedure stalled, the Third Estate met alone and formally adopted the title of National Assembly; three days later, they met in a nearby indoor tennis court and took the so-called Tennis Court Oath vowing not to disperse until constitutional reform had been achieved. Within a week, most of the clerical deputies and 47 liberal nobles had joined them, and on June 27 louis XVI grudgingly absorbed all three orders into the new National Assembly.

The Bastille

On June 12, as the National Assembly (known as the National Constituent Assembly during its work on a constitution) continued to meet at Versailles, fear and violence consumed the capital. Though, enthusiastic about the recent breakdown of the royal power, Parisians grew panicked as rumors of an impending military coup began to circulate. A popular insurgency culminated on July 14 when rioters stormed the Bastille fortress in an attempt to secure gunpowder and weapons. The wave of revolutionary fervor and widespread hysteria quickly swept the entire country. Revolting against years of exploitation, peasants looted and burned the homes of tax collectors, landlords and the aristocratic elite. Known as the great Fear, the agrarian insurrection hastened the growing exodus of nobles from France and inspired the National Constituent

Assembly to abolish feudalism on August 4, 1789, signing what historian Georges Lefebvre later called the "death certificate of the old order.

Declaration of the Rights of Man and of the Citizen

In late August, the Assembly adopted the Declaration of the Rights of Man and of the Citizen, statement of democratic principles grounded in the philosophical and political ideas of Enlightenment thinkers like Jean Jacques Rousseau. The document proclaimed the Assembly's commitment to replace the ancient regime with a system based on equal opportunity, freedom of speech, popular sovereignty and representative government. Drafting a formal constitution proved much more of a challenge for the National Constituent Assembly, which had the added burden of functioning as a legislature during harsh economic times.

Adopted on September 3, 1791, France's first written constitution echoed the more moderate voices in the Assembly, establishing a constitutional monarchy in which the king enjoyed royal veto power and the ability to appoint ministers. This compromise did not set well with influential radicals like Maximilien de Robespierre, Camille Desmoulins and Georges Danton, who began drumming up popular support for a more republican form of government and for the trial of louis XVI.

French Revolution Turns Radical

In April 1792, the newly elected Legislative Assembly declared War on Austria and Prussia, where it believed that French emigres were building counterrevolutionary alliances; it also hoped to spread its revolutionary ideals across Europe through warfare. On the domestic front, meanwhile, the political crisis took a radical turn when a group of insurgents led by the extremist Jacobins attacked the royal residence in Paris and arrested the King on August 10, 1792. The following month, amid a wave of violence in which Parisian insurrectionists massacred hundreds of accused counterrevolutionaries, the Legislative Assembly was replaced by the National Convention, which proclaimed the abolition of the monarchy and the establishment of the French republic. On January 21, 1793, it sent king Louis XVI, condemned to death for high treason and crimes against the state, to the guillotine; his wife Marie-Antoinette suffered the same fate nine month later.

French Revolution Ends: Napoleon's Rise:

The Directory's four years in power were riddled with financial crises, popular discontent, inefficiency and, above all, political corruption. By the late 1790s, the directors relied almost entirely on the military to maintain their authority and had ceded much of their power to the generals in the field. On November 9, 1799, as frustration with their leadership reached a fever pitch, Napoleon Bonaparte staged a coup d'etat, abolishing the Directory and appointing himself France's "first consul." The event marked the end of the French Revolution and the beginning of the Napoleonic era, during which France would come to dominate much of continental Europe.

The aftermath effect of the French revolution resulted to the establishment of a democratic system in France and led to most European countries adopting the system of governance and also spreading to other part of North American countries and its colonies. This event certainly did not put end to revolution as another event took a wave in the 21 century when the Arab Spring engulfed the Arab countries.

ARAB SPRING

Arab Spring, wave of pro-democracy protests and uprisings that took place in the Middle East and North Africa beginning in 2010 and 2011, challenging some of the region's entrenched authoritarian regimes. The wave began when protests in Tunisia and Egypt toppled their regimes in quick succession, inspiring similar attempts in other Arab countries. Not every country saw success in the protest movement, however, and demonstrators expressing their political and economic grievances were often met with violent crackdowns by their countries' security forces.

Two countries will be filtered from this revolutionary event that narrates the impact of leadership in crises and revolution management in succumbing to the will of the people to avoid havoc and destruction of national asset. These countries are Tunisia and Libya:

Tunisia's Jasmine Revolution

The first demonstrations took place in central Tunisia in central Tunisia in December 2010, catalyzed by the self-immolation of Mohamed Bouazizi, a 26-year-old street vendor protesting his treatment by local officials. A protest movement, dubbed the "Jasmine Revolution" in the media, quickly spread through the country. The Tunisian government attempted to end the unrest by using violence against street demonstrations and by offering political and economic concessions. However, protests soon overwhelmed the country's security forces, compelling Pres. Zine al-Abidine Ben Ali to step down and flee the country on January 14, 2011. In October 2011, Tunisians participated in a free election to choose members of a council tasked with drafting a new constitution. A democratically chosen president and prime minister took office in December 2011, and a new constitution was promulgated in January 2014. In

October-November 2019, Tunisia became the first country of the Arab Spring protests to undergo a peaceful transfer of power from one democratically elected government to another.

Libya Revolution

The Libya protests against the regime of Muammar al-Qaddafi in mid-February 2011 quickly escalated into an armed revolt. When the rebel forces appeared to be on the verge of defeat in March, an international coalition led by NATO launched a campaign of air strikes targeting Qaddafi's forces. Although NATO intervention ultimately shifted the military balance in favour of the rebel forces, Qaddafi was able to cling to power in the capital, Tripoli, for several more months. He was forced from power in August 2011 after rebel forces took control of Tripoli. After evading capture for several weeks., Qaddafi was killed in Sirte in October 2011 as rebel forces took control of the city. A transitional National Council, set up by rebel forces and recognized internationally, took power, but its struggle to exert authority over the country precipitated the outbreak of civil war in 2014.

Analysis of The Uprising

The outcome of the Libyan revolution is a tale of leadership and organizational impacts in the event. The North Africa nation is confined within the African continent; and a member of the African Union (AU) whom proposedly is responsible for overseeing the continental affairs even though Libya is recognized as a former French colony "a member of NATO". Was NATO appropriate to have executed an attack on Libya soil? If allied military intervention is to get involve in the revolution; was the African Union, the Arab League and the United Nations not in appropriate positions to have mediated between the Libyan leaders and the rebels in a move to swiftly put an end to the revolution which precedes to the Civil war. International organization such as the United Nations must assumed it roles as a global body in averting wars, revolutions and conflicts between member states, and at situation where it deem necessary to involve other continental allies in reaching an absolute conclusion in the resolution of an incident; then the United Nations, being a security council of member states should not hesitate on measures on restoring and sustaining peace between warring parties of member states. If wars and revolution persist at a time when it shouldn't, especially at a time of multitude organizations whose expectancies are to balance the affairs of member states; then the leadership circle in these organizations simply need to reevaluate the effectiveness of their roles on member states. The Tunisia scenario showcase the effectiveness of the leadership role in a democratic dispensation for respect for the will of the people to prevail. The prompt decision by the president to step down dose the demonstration and agitation of the protesters and averted a situation that could have escalated into the Libyan scenario; and alongside paving way for the democratic institution to reform and draft the constitution with the election of a new president and prime minister to office in December 2011. The resolution of the Tunisia revolution reveals the measure of strength of a leader by not being the ability to cling to authorities when the country is at the path to disaster, but the ability to let go of authorities for the will of the people and for the betterment of the nation, which was otherwise the case of Libya.

Conflicts and Nations Building

Conflicts and revolutions cannot be excepted from nations polity, though bad as it seems, it attributes to a more effective nation does not shrug off its significance for the emergence of nations to align to the modern world. At the modern time of civility, nations should be mindful of governance and its roles and the political mediators that are responsible for the affairs of nations. Conflicts and revolutions are resolute outcome from agitation for better policies in public services that the people derive from. The will of the people should not just prevail, the will of the majority should stand out. The idealism of conflicts and revolutions pertaining to nation state is somewhat subjected to mass demonstrations and protests in regards to a stimulus that have to do with the people's wellbeing, and this idealism is attached to the intellectual capacities and level of enlightenment of the people and the leaders. The necessities of demonstrations are expression of dissatisfaction and awareness to governance and the political elites on issues affecting the people's welfare. Political conflicts are common in politics, and when not propelling managed, escalate to revolution that somewhat translate to destruction of national assets, and further degrade the integrity of the governing council. Whereas, on the other hand, constructive conflicts of the political establishment can enhance national development which is the products of pollical thoughts and intellectual capacities of the people and the nation.

Conflict, therefore, can be defined as perceived threat to individual values and way of life that altered the social wellbeing of living (Akanni 2022). It is ideal in a dynamic world that situations and ways of life get transformed either positively or negatively due to subsequent changes in the world's affairs in the economic, political, and social aspect of life. In politics, this plays out in a range of ways; in some cases, parties will agree on goals but disagree on how to achieve them, and in other cases, parties will disagree on goals, sometimes parties will not agree on the facts to the dispute obscuring any potential for problem-solving. In practice, there are two fundamental types of conflict: constructive conflicts and destructive conflicts.

    (i) **Constructive conflicts:** These are conflicts that generate positive outcomes and problem-solving. Political conflicts are constructive when the challenges between parties are met with resolution that exceed the status quo. The interests, values, and needs of the parties can be assessed in terms of three satisfactions: process, emotion, and substance. The process dimension includes features of acknowledgement and inclusion. The emotional dimension captures a range of feelings as they relate to engagement, identity, safety, and security. As emotions are processed, they can illuminate issues, and what starts as anger may turn into fear. Fear, in turn, tends to reflect clear underlying interests and needs and the address them. The substantive concerns are the tangible components of the conflict. Politics that are expressed as issues of equitable distribution of resources may be experienced by parties as existential threats. One group's "fair" may not serve as another group's "survival." The constructive version of these types of problems sees the needs of both (all) sides being met, and, in turn, this reduces the potential for costly escalations in violence and results in a net gain.

(j) **Destructive conflict:** When conflicts increase the dysfunction in relationships between parties and antagonize or inflame processes making the possibility of reaching resolution or achieving a settlement, they can be described as destructive. In politics, destructive conflicts can sometimes have a life of their own or may blow up. Exposing one issue may reveal a larger pattern, system, or history of antagonisms, distrust, or failed dispute resolution processes. Rather than becoming informed and cooperative when disagreement surfaces parties in destructive conflicts begin to dig in and commit to adversarial process dynamics.

In politics this can get exaggerated, and questions about morale, motivation, and public image can escalate to existential threats, hyperbole, and generalized prejudice in the name of biases and attribution errors. Political expedience and political conflicts are frequently disengaged from the truth in favor of distorted narratives designed in favor of biased political agendas.

Revolution and Nation Building

A nation presumably is a special form of political community associated historically, and (if properly defined) logically with the institution of the state. It is as we know opposed both in history and logic to empire. Its principle of cohesion is nationalism – a degree of consciousness of separateness and high valuation of political autonomy. Nation building is presumably then a metaphoric rubric for the social process or processes by which national consciousness appears in certain groups which through a social structure – more or less institutionalize – act to attain political autonomy for their society.

Nationalism, in its ideological manifestation, is an assertion of the right of a people – however distinguished

– to determine its political destiny autonomously. It is merely an assertion of value to be made good in this case by a persuasive political dialectic. Political dialectics are not, for the most part, a simply conversations. They are matters of political action by more or less organized groups of people. Political dialectics are dialogues of power. Nationalism implies democracy in the sense of public participation in politics since its assertion of basic political right in self-determination. The sources of power supporting the assertion of this right, if they are any, would presumably be the organization of the populace for, political action.

Among others, Karl Deutsch has drawn out attention to a process which he calls social mobilization. An effective national political community must be well up on the scales of social mobilization. **Revolution** is understood as a method of political struggle wage primarily on the basis of mobilization of energies latent in a certain kind of society and organized and routinized can be considered a concrete example of nation building in process. This kind of struggle, characteristically, can turn on the mobilization and organization of the population. In the pre-revolutionary state these populations are politically immobile and passive. The configuration of societies as they exist in pre-revolutionary state of affairs contains a substantial 'gap' between the urban and rural segments.

The existence of the 'gap' along many dimensions of social structure has been widely noted in the literature of underdeveloped societies; it seems to be the resultant of the process of modernization. This gap, a point of weakness or fragility of the social structures of such societies, is the key to the kind of revolution.

The aspect of gap is characteristic of the rural-agrarian segment which we can call its immobility, or better, its quality of being immobilized. This refers to several sub-characteristics such as economic immobility (underemployment), civil immobility (lack of political participation), status immobility (caste), psychic immobility (superstition). In other words, the "gap" is immobility along scales of a variety of values. Now it is into this gap of immobility that the revolution breaks with its organizing apparatus. In its ideal development it mobilizes the immobilized energies of the rural population with a set of organizations and draws them into a great structure of activity.

To the extent that this process of mobilization succeeds, the revolutionary movement becomes that much impenetrable and irreversible, because the mobilization process both uses human energy more fully and also educates the participants to an understanding of new frames of mind, new beliefs, and new social organizations. To carry out such mobilization effectively demands resources of leadership with administrative ability. The communication of a charisma or set of sympathetic symbols has received attention as an effective leadership device to arouse responsiveness in populations of underdeveloped societies. A great deal of effort is directed toward the "routinization" of a charismatic or symbolic penetration of the masses by building strong organizations.

In order to accomplish this task, people of skills are necessary; it is for this reason as much as any, that the revolution seeks to attract the intelligentsia in the societies. The tactical use of national fronts, party alliances, and analyses of class interests is directed to the problem of recruiting intelligentsia. Such devises justify support and participation from privileged classes in activities which are more or less openly aimed at the ostensible elimination of privilege, while explaining the division of educated classes into conflicting groups. It is notable that revolution, to be successful and to be carried through to a new state of stability, must attract the support of a sizeable number of educated people. More specifically, however, is the conduct of political activity- particularly revolution – the capacity on a great variety of activities in a coordinated manner is extraordinarily valuable. Revolutionary activity demands the capacity to sustain a tempo of development of military, agitational, and administrative work as well as the defensive capacity to withdraw intact in the face of tactical failure.

The aim of the revolution is to annihilate constituted authority and substitute a new authority. The simultaneity of these two aspects of the process may be critical in successful nation building. The process of annihilation is pursued by actions which on one hand seek to demonstrate the ineffectiveness of constituted authority – such acts as sabotage, terrorism, armed raids, ambushes, and the like – and on the other hand to destroy the concept of justice upon which constituted authority stands, by such acts as propaganda attacks on land law and other economic relationships, on the honesty and integrity of officials, on the patriotism of officials, and on the justice social relations and social opportunities.

The concrete conditions which mold the content of revolutionary attacks vary from situation to situation. The revolution is able to adapt pragmatically to these conditions because of its elaborate organization, which places political officers and workers in the smallest group. Constituted authority, by virtue of its being established, is largely bound to the conditions being attacked; its flexibility of response has several limitations. The first limit is what might be termed an inherent obtuseness. Constituted authority finds it very difficult to perceive any aspects of its position as unjust. Yet any system of authority can be explained in terms that make it seem unjust. Secondly, the constituted authority has a variety of positions both geographical and moral which it must defend, and therefore many of its resources are occupied in defense against potential attack. Finally, constituted authority, being better supplied and equipped, is likely to have made prior choices about organization, logistics, and tactics which commit it to certain directions to the exclusion of others.

In order that a revolutionary struggle may go forward it is necessary to disrupt existing structure of authority. It is a striking fact that in those areas where the revolution was carried through to a resolution satisfactory to the revolutionaries, the traditional authority had been severely disrupted before the revolution. The techniques of terrorism against authority's personnel, combined with other destructive activity (destroying crops, communications, and other property), certainly might increase the general state of insecurity sufficiently to stimulate anxiety and erode the basis of authority in the psychological acceptance of it as effective. At the same time propaganda aimed at symbolizing the government as unjust, corrupt, and alien could match the subversion of the acceptance of authority's effectiveness with a conscious rejection of its justice.

The revolution organization is ready to substitute authority for that annihilated. As soon as the opportunity arises, new governmental institutions at the local, intermediate, and national levels are established. These institutions will produce policies which initially should probably be understood as part of the attacks on established authority, since they will suggest to the people the feasibility of alternative social, economic, and political relations. But as the process goes forward, they can constitute an emerging national entity.

Several characteristics of warfare are notable within the context of processes of political change. Warfare is some form is known in almost all cultures. Considered as such it may be prosecuted in more or less sophisticated forms but it is a familiar phenomenon. In addition, the techniques of warfare are relatively simple. At the guerilla level, they remain so since the technological primitive people, can very soon become adept in the use of small arms. Finally, the place of war in the cultural structure of pleasant peoples is marginal. It is less likely, particularly in modernizing societies characterized by the "gap" mentioned before, to be deeply involved in rigid traditional social structures. Therefore, warfare might be termed a conceptually familiar and socially flexible activity which can in practice move people from one kind of social structure to another by way of "emergency" measures and practices which continue ostensibly only "for the duration."

The relationship between certain characteristics of underdeveloped agrarian societies and guerrilla warfare techniques common in revolutionary war is quite clear. For example, the existence of widespread peasant agricultural of a quasi-subsistence type makes the logistics of food and other personal needs of guerrilla troops relatively simple. Moreover, the heavy concentration of rural population, together with characteristic rural underemployment, provides a reservoir of manpower from which combatants and service personnel can be recruited. The primitiveness of communications also gives the guerrillas an advantage over organized troop units that may be vastly stronger over all, but are mechanized, dependent on more complex logistics, and required to defend the lifelines of urban elements of the society. These characteristics merely permit guerrilla activities to be maintained, however; despite their advantages, it appears highly improbable that guerrillas can do anything decisive to the main elements of an organized military force. Guerrilla warfare, if it is to amount to anything more than banditry, must therefore become part of a combined activity.

In revolutionary war, the guerrilla forces serve a central function. This mobilization process of the revolution seems to be critically distinguishing feature of revolutionary war as a model of political conflict. The potentialities of mobilization are also peculiarly characteristic of underdeveloped agrarian societies.

LEADERSHIP, THE KEY TO TRANSFORMATION

Man is the greatest resource society can portray, because he is instilled with abilities and frame of mind to have activities within its environs in control. "leadership is a process of time mold by the environment", to large extent, the people are determinant to the caliber of leaders it places at helm of affairs. Countries have experienced different styles of leadership, imperialism, parliamentary, and foreign sovereignty-oriented leadership. The tedious part of any democratic formation is the procedure for selection of leaders which is often given serious attention through a systematic process. In the system, the people are empowered by the constitution the freedom to freely choose those who govern their affairs, while those who are elected must be accountable by ensuring that everyone is equal before the law and actual ability determines who is put in positions of public responsibility.

Leadership roles in the stability of nations is significant in nation building and national development. Leaders qualities is not only measured by abilities to enhance national development and wellbeing of the people; its strength is measured during difficulties and conflicts in the political system, how challenges are overcome and how public opinions that emanated from critical aspect of public issues are resolved without necessarily escalating to national or political conflict. Two incidents were aforementioned pertaining to the roles of leadership in the Arab uprising citing Tunisia and Libya.

The Tunisia president at the wake of the uprising quickly responded siting the threat it poses to peace in the country political establishment and other Arab nations and the possibility of escalating into revolution which could claim lives and destruction of national assets; to avert the threat, he swiftly considered the political option of easing the seat to douse the tension and create space for the democratic formation to yields to the public issues that prompted the uprising which actually led to democratic institution to reform and draft the constitution with the election of a new president and prime minister to office in December 2011. The resolution of the Tunisia revolution reveals the measure of strength of a leader by not being the ability to cling to authorities when the country is at the path to disaster, but the ability to let go of authorities for the will of the people to prevail for the betterment of the nation.

The Libyan leader response is more of self-eccentric rather than the people centric approach of his Tunisia counterpart. Though, while I acknowledged the Libyan leader agitation and push for a viable African economy with his strategic plan to establish a common currency for the continent that will drive and propel the Africa growth and exchange policies globally as adopted by the European counterpart was condemned and perceived as not applicable to the continent by the West and some African nations. His approach is to unify the African economy to a single entity to have a common economical formation. An idea that exist in a person without the acceptance of the majority is not to be nurtured or respect attached to the person. Such was the case of Muammar al-Qaddafi in the continent and the African Union. Though, his prolonged years of administration in the country is acknowledged and could be a decisive factor while the idea was jettison and the reason for accumulated grievances ignited the Arab uprising. The strength of leaders is knowing when to act and when not to. The Libya revolution could have been mediated and acted upon by the continental African Union whose responsibility it is to oversee the political affairs of member state rather than an external military intervention by 'NATO' in the revolution. Perhaps, I thought, maybe the reason he clings to authority was to push his ideology to actualization in the continent before he eases off the political arena. Above all, blames remained his, he could have taken time off the political arena to push forth his ideas in the continent. Position of authority are crucial just as the purpose it is for. The Libya narrative is the aftermath of structural democratic system not formally defined by pattern at which it expected respective leaders to function in regards authority and duration. When they are a clear constitutional narrative for an established entity, its appropriate leadership roles.

Therefore, **Leadership** is the coordination and administration of man and land resource for the development of all components in its vicinity, (Akanni 2020). It is optimizing substantial resources to effect transformation within domain of one's role. Leadership can either be understood as a pattern of behavior or a personal quality. As a patten of behavior, leadership is the influence exerted by an individual or group over a large body to organize or direct its efforts towards the achievement of desired goals. As a personal attitude, leadership refers to the character traits which enable the leader to exert influence over others. Leadership in both pattern of behavior and personal quality are both implemented in conducts of affairs either personal or in collective. Ironically, both are exhibited through administration of behavior to effect impacts on whatever it is applied to. **Administration** on the other hand, are actions modeled towards institutions on how it should operate and function, (Akanni 2022). Hence, the key points in the definition, "coordination and administration of man and resources", matched by personal attribute of the leader in any circumference. We can't refer to effective leadership without considering the administrative qualities and skills, as this is what attribute to behavioral influence in its roles, especially, when it has to do with governance. Leadership in governance is embodied by public administration of government assets, which are the territory, resources and the people.

Public administration is a cadre of governance at various level of public policies implementation for the management of public sectors that enhances public services for the beneficiary of the people, (Akanni 2022). The fundamental goal is to advance management and policies so that government can function. A leader, in whatever capacities, must possess the following qualities of public administrator:

Qualities of Public Administrator

1. **Commitment to vision:** When the administrator is enthused about the organization or agency's mission, the employees will mirror those feelings. In times of crisis, great administrators remind their staff of the purpose of their mission and the role their organization plays in the larger society.
2. **Strategic Vision:** Public administrators must always remain focused on the strategic vision and

the long-term mission of the agency or organization. Staff members are expected to be aware with the mode of operations of the agency, to understand and align to future plans. It is important to remember that the agency or organization was often around long before the public administration arrived, and will remain in operation long after the administrator leaves.

3. **Conceptual skill:** Leaders must always be able to see how anyone action or decision affects every part of the company or organization. Staff members may only see as far as their department or shift; leaders must always see beyond those limits.

4. **Attention to detail:** One quality of an administrator is to see the big picture and think strategically. However, it is equally important for effective administrators to pay attention to details. This does not mean leaders must be involved in every minor decision, or undermine the decisions of subordinates; rather, leaders must remain aware of the activities of their staff and the status of projects, allowing autonomy whenever possible.

5. **Delegation:** there is a fine line between delegating tasks to staff and shirking from responsibilities, knowing subordinates will take

up the slack. Great public administrators navigate this distinction by assigning not just tasks, but clearly defined spheres of influence where staff members have the authority to make decisions. Delegating tasks and responsibilities in this manner empowers staff members to grow in their positions, preparing them for future leadership positions.

6. **Growth mindset:** A public administrator must be able to take existing talent within the organization, nurture it, and place staff members in positions where they can be successful. Public must be mindful not to stifle growth by becoming overbearing or forcing staff members into positions for which they are ill-suited.

7. **Hiring Savvy:** Many people enter public service because they have a deep desire to make their community a better place; however, desire and skill do not necessarily go hand in hand. Public administrators can set their agency or organization up for success from the very beginning by hiring the right people, for the right jobs, at the right time. Great administrators take measured risks, knowing that one bad hire can have negative ripple effects on the organization.

8. **Emotional balance:** Almost every person experiences deep emotions at one time or another, and those emotions can be harnessed for good or ill by leaders. Great leaders funnel emotions, such as rage, anger, and happiness, into positive action that drives change. Poor leaders use emotions as an excuse to lash out at staff members, creating uncomfortable working conditions.
9. **Creativity:** In most circumstances, public administrators work on shoestring budgets with short deadlines and difficult, seemingly impossible objectives. Another quality of an administrator is to thrive on those unique challenges and use the restrictions as a way to showcase their creativity. Public administrators are able to come up with creative solutions to complex problems, usually by seeing an issue from a new perspective or by innovating a new approach to the solution.
10. **Digital communication and social expertise:** Public administrators largely work for the people of a community and may be held accountable for their actions at any time. Successful administrators exhibit excellent digital

communication skills, especially communication via social media.

11. **Communication skills:** Good communication skills help public leaders in several overarching ways. An agency that communicates information and expectations clearly, both internally and externally, runs efficiently and accomplishes more. Proper communication also aids in transparency which is an important quality for organizations that operate in the public eye.

    On the flip side, poor communication can reduce efficiency, which can hamper an organization's effectiveness. Lack of transparency can promote public suspicion and cause problems where none actually exist. By learning good communication skills and practicing them every day, public leaders can avoid these pitfalls and guide their agencies to success.

12. **Public engagement:** As essential quality of an administrator is to cultivate public engagement. To support policy development activities, government and nonprofit leaders must engage the public and keep them well informed about what is happening in the organization. Proper communication in these categories reap many benefits.

- Citizens who are well informed about a policy that is being implemented are more likely to react according to public administration expectations.
- Citizens' opinions about policy issues are based on reliable knowledge instead of negative emotions.
- Citizens know their rights and responsibilities in the legislative process.
- Citizens understand how they can benefit from and access proposed social programs.
- An organization can avoid having a negative public policy opinion turn into a crisis situation, which in turn will save time and money.

Informed citizens are clearly better partners. By fostering this relationship, public administrators who are good communicators both serve the public, and make their own jobs easier and more effective.

In every sphere, leadership has significant impact in meeting defined purpose and objectives. Firstly, to meet the purpose of the roles, and then the objectives of the organizational establishment. Leadership in governance primarily, is to stabilize fair living conditions for the people and wellbeing of the nation that enhances national development and sustainability. Nations with this structural operational pattern forms the basis for a profound administrative system in public service deliveries. When public service deliveries match the expectation of the citizens that no one is deprived of any benefits, then a country can be regarded as developed. The gap between developed nations and the third world countries "underdeveloped nations" are obvious in the public services and conditions of living of the citizens. Underdeveloped nations also have the potentials to be developed, all they need do is to establish an atmosphere where the factors responsible for underdevelopment can gradually be undo towards the path to development; which can only be done by critically understanding and analysis the features attached to the undeveloped status. Features of underdeveloped nations:

Features of Underdeveloped Nations

(1) **Bad Governance:** Bad governance is the failure to appropriate and account for the utility of availed resources to effect nation building by the leading elites, (Akanni 2020). It is regarded as lack of compassion and patriotism to enhance growth and development in ones' capacity, and mostly driven with eccentric desires to fulfill self-interest. This, no doubt, has lay many developing

nations low on worth, and it causes is not farfetched from the few factors which are:

- **High proportion of illiteracy:** This is a scenario where large proportion of the population lack basic education necessary to make them responsive citizens. The impact of education in a country's affair is vast; and its importance to the development of nations is stressed along application of knowledge which in turn reflect in the political elites. Providing basic educational amenities is the responsibility of governance and a shortfall of it in the nation is a failure on the political class.
- **Lack of mutual understanding:** An egalitarian society is one that regards is attached to everyone irrespective of their ethnic linings. Any nations where there is discord or disregards amongst the people, it will be difficult for such nation to form a progressive body or ideologies to propel the country.
- **Ethnocentrism:** This is the idea of supremacy that exist between cultural and tribal groups which often come into play in terms of leadership in the political arena instead of the most qualified candidates being the decisive factor in the

electioneering process of selecting the leader of the nation.

- **Indiscipline:** The effectiveness of any organization or countries progress is adherence to the code of conducts modeled to the operations and functionalities of the institutions. If there is a deviant from the organizational conducts, it creates lapses in the productivity of the institutions affecting deliverables in return.
- **Poverty:** This is a large proportion of the population living below the established benchmark of the economy on expected income of individual persons. It is a situation where the population overstretched the available resources.

(2) **Lack of requisites knowledge and skills:** Since leadership is about administration of organizational affairs ranging from people to resources. Anyone who is to assume position of authority in governance must first have gone through a systematic behavioral formulation process and then must have had opportunities of exhibiting such experiences in endeavors of profession to be able to handle activities of the country effectively without much difficulties. This is a peculiar issue with the third world nations as

most of its leaders lack requisites knowledge and skills to effect transformation in their countries. When a leader is sound in knowledge, propelling national development and sustainability will not be much of a task.

(3) **Lack of maturity to withstand challenges:** All leaders must have it share of displeasures from both constructive and destructive criticisms from the public or political rivals on pattern of administration on public issues that affect the people's wellbeing. When criticisms are laid out, it is mostly to attract the awareness of the political elites on vital points that are pertaining to public issues. This are mostly challenging time for leaders psychological as it stained their wellbeing to withstand difficulties, and their strength in overcoming it. Most conflicts and political crisis from developing nations have emanated from lack of intellectual capacities to process the criticism constructively to withstand the political pressure, identify the basic issues and proffer way forward for resolution.

(4) **Desire for dominance:** A well formatted democratic dispensation is the system that operate with periodical stipulating specific duration administration ought to end. What its

aid is new ideologies on how to administer the countries affairs. Leaders in the developing countries are reckoned with desire to cling to authority for long duration of time living the economy and sustenance of the nation rigid to their time. Most often, they are authoritarian in nature and largely fail to synergize with the governing body to identify and address vital societal needs.

(5) **Disconnection between the four arms of governance:** As we are aware, all democratic system consists (i) the executive (ii) the legislative (iii) the judiciary (iv) the citizens; for it to be regarded as one. And a propel dispensation synergies with the arms for a profound egalitarian nation where respect for all is acknowledged. When they are discord between the arms, disparity and inequalities would certainly manifest creating disconnection between the governance and the people. The implication of this is that, governance loses touch with citizens and the system, and the essence of governance and its integrity is lost.

(6) **Political ethnocentrism:** is the ideology of supremacy that exist between political bodies basically established and emboldened by the

electoral act with primary role of candidate selection for political positions in the electoral process, (Akanni 2020). The affiliation of political bodies/parties is a common exercise among citizens as they pinch tent to different wings during selection process. For a multiethnic society in adversities, the forming of political parties is mostly aligned to tribal lines and cultural ideologies causing fixation to ones' ethnic linings against competencies in the electoral process.

It is evident that the quality of leadership determines the quality of governance, and governance is fully derived when its beneficial to the people. There is a distinction between leadership and the citizenship who adheres and follows the policies established by the leading elites. The effectiveness of leadership is derived from followers; to understand the impact of their roles in any formation, it is important to have the interpretation of their roles in the impacts on followership in any organizational setting.

When working as a team, some people naturally take leadership role while others provide support as followers. Both roles are essential for successful collaboration within a group. Being a leader or a follower may come naturally to some people while others have to learn how to fulfill their place on their team. Learning how to be a good follower can contribute to your teamwork skills and provide a useful perspective for future leadership opportunities.

Followership is the ability to accomplish goals under a leader's direction. Successful followership involves following instructions, completing assigned tasks, supporting initiatives and being motivated. Good followers see the value in listening to others and helping achieve their vision. Followership in the workplace emphasizes holding oneself to high standard of personal success while contributing to the overall benefit of the team. Some of the qualities that can help succeed in the workplace:

Qualities of Followers

(1) **Ego management**: Good followers have their egos under control. They are team players in the truest sense of the concept. They have good interpersonal skills and display empathy. A good follower success relates more to performance and goal achievement rather than personal recognition and self-promotion.

(2) **Loyalty:** Good followers respect their obligation to be loyal to their employer. Followers who are not loyal are more likely to create problems between team members, compromise goal

achievement and reduce the team's productivity. As a follower, you have a strong allegiance and commitment to the company's plans. You know that your obligations are to the company, not a given leader at a given point in time.

(3) **Humility:** The ability to show humility is an important part of effective followership. Help others find opportunities where they can lead and respect their authority promotes a culture of shared professional growth in the workplace. You acknowledge when others have great ideas and are proactive about supporting their efforts. Also understanding the importance of contribution to project, regardless of how simple or complicated it is. When a leader assigns tasks, respect is attached to the roles of others on your team.

(4) **Work ethic:** Team function best when leaders and followers are dedicated to a project. Strong followers are motivated to excel even when they are not specifically in charge of the project. Through actions, one can demonstrate that you are diligent, committed and pay attention to detail. These are the same qualities that leaders will look for when it comes to time for promotions or other leadership opportunities offer.

(5) **Courage:** Followers must take direction but they also have an underlying obligation to do so only when the direction is ethical and proper. Followership means having the courage to speak up when you have concerns. The role may also require to give negative feedback to leader or other team members.

(6) **Active listening:** Active listening is a core aspect of followership because it promotes understanding between team members. By engaging others with questions or clarifying comments, you can establish clear expectations for your own duties. Active listening helps one understand a leader's strategies and suggestions, which then gives the knowledge and motivation to thrive. Show active listening in the workplace by paying attention during meetings, asking for input from others and regularly checking it with team members about shared goals.

(7) **Tact:** Sharing your ideas in a group setting while acknowledging a leader's choice involves using emotional intelligence, interpersonal awareness and tact. As leaders share their ideas, one may show appreciation for their guidance and address any concerns in a manner that focuses on finding solutions. Be prepared to give an honest

assessment of what the leader is trying to achieve. Good leaders are grateful for constructive feedback from their team.

(8) **Teamwork:** Successful followership requires strong teamwork skills and a group-oriented mindset. Demonstrating teamwork as a follower involves working hard, being fair with others and offering your assistance when team members need help. Promoting synergy within a group makes it easier to accomplish objectives, share support and solve problems as a team. Your loyalty to the team's mission and the leader's vision can influence workplace efficiency and operations.

(9) **Good judgement:** It is just as important for a follower to have good judgement as a leader. If leaders know they can depend on followers to do high-quality, timely work, they may give more responsibilities and independence. If good judgement is shown as a follower, it may provide an opportunity to lead in the future.

(10) **Adaptability:** For a team to operate successfully, members may need to adopt multiple roles and be flexible in their duties. Positive followership involves a willingness to assist with incomplete tasks and adjust work

strategy to meet team objectives. Adaptability makes a better follower and makes entire team more willing to approach large projects. Showing adaptability as a follower also exposes to multiple types of responsibilities and prepares for future leadership opportunities.

(11) **Competency:** While followership emphasizes teamwork, good followers also have a high level of competency. Being a follower who drives progress on a team involves knowing how to do a job well and independently completing delegated tasks. You can use followership skills to interpret direction and guidance from a leader while using specialized knowledge to determine the best way to accomplish assignments.

(12) **Critical thinking:** Well-functioning teams include both followers and leaders thinking critically about how their actions influence outcomes and goals. Critical thinking supports ability to contribute to team goals and give useful feedback to team leaders. It improves judgement and understanding on full context of how a team interacts and works together. Promote followership with critical thinking by using good judgement and being thoughtful about how choices in the workplace support team success.

(13) **Attention to detail:** Leadership involves envisioning overarching, long-term goals while followership focuses on completing the detailed steps to achieve those objectives. Paying attention to detail and caring about the technical aspects of a project ensures thorough, quality work. Detail-oriented people can thrive in a followership role because they can dedicate their time and attention to high-level tasks while the leader manages workflows and compiles each element into a final project.

(14) **Time management:** When leaders give directions and delegates tasks, they rely on committed followers to accomplish those goals according to schedule. Followership requires an understanding of time management strategies so you can organize tasks and meet expectations.

The concept of leadership is germane to nation building. It is believed that no society can rise above the quality of its leader. "if we have mediocre leaders don't expect high class development strategies." The need for leaders who have vision, mission, courage, empathy, listening ears, sensitivity and spiritual insight to move nations forward are what show be at the forefront during the selection process of electioneering. Exemplary leadership therefore can be relevant in nation building when it is manifested in representative governance which endorses electoral processes that are free, fair, credible and transparent.

Exemplary leadership is devoid of any instances of oppression, repression, exploitation, inhuman and unpatriotic interactions in the leaders and the citizens. He identifies truth, good reputation, and respect for justice; sound character and integrity with knowledge as basic ingredients of good leadership that will build a nation. Leadership with clear vision, leadership with legitimate authority and decisive leadership augur well for nation building.

Attributes of Exemplary Leadership

1. **Confidence:** Great leaders are looked upon by the people they lead as figures of trust and reliability. A good leader must possess and display confidence in order to reassure and inspire those below him. It is imperative to look knowledgeable and competent and appear unperturbed by the trials that will arise. One cannot expect to inspire confidence in others if he is hesitant and unsure.
2. **Character:** A leader's character must be exemplary; otherwise his credibility is

undermined and he will lose respect from those who are supposed to follow. Character can be defined as possessing and manifestly displaying virtues such as trustworthiness, honesty, kindness, generosity and fairness. You must lead by example, and if your example is poor it will reflect on the organization.

3. **Intelligence:** A leader lacking intelligence is hard to respect., both for those he leads and for the world in general. He needs to be able to act with wisdom and make decisions that are beneficial to the organization and those within it. Without intelligence he is incapable of attaining excellence either personally or for the organization he leads.

4. **Passion:** An exemplary leader feels and displays passion and enthusiasm for the role and the general purpose to which his leadership is directed, whether he is general defeating an enemy or a business leader getting the best work performance out of his team members. Great leadership is not only about technical ability and competence but also about emotion. Human beings are emotional creatures at heart and react to

emotional appeals and influences. If a leader is passionate about the task before him, he is more likely to be able to generate positive emotional responses in his constituency.

VALUES, THE COMPONENT TO ENHANCING NATION BUILDING

Humans have the unique ability to describe their identity, select their values and set up their beliefs. All three of these directly persuade a person's behavior. Values are our principles and guides. Morals and the values are the basis of human values.

Values are doctrine of worth placed on self. It is stimulated by one's internalized beliefs and knowledge acquired from various endeavors, and it determines responses and reaction to stimuli, (Akanni 2020). A country's worth is measured by the value it places on its citizens; and a country's progress is determined by the value citizens placed on it. The destiny of a country is profound in the people, while values are yardstick for enhancing nation building as it serves as the channel to establishing egalitarian society that encourages and preserves equality for all. Values formed the backbone for moral compass and behavior formulation that propels human interaction in the environment. Human interaction is not limited to itself; it unifies all societal components and conformed to standards formulated as ethical conducts with expectancy of adherence.

Nation building is the combination of willingness, determination and utility of availed resources for the development and growth of the vicinity, (Akanni 2020). It is the foundation of purposefulness a nation earmarked to accomplish with commitment of its resources that emanate from willingness of adding value to its identity. Values are standards for effective leadership and good governance, and when it comes to nation building, it is the behavioral and cultural values indoctrinated by societal components in creation of a common purpose; as it does with bad governance with deficient values that often leads to social vices denigrating societal worth. Contemporary crisis in issues as:

(i) Corruption
(ii) Robbery
(iii) Kidnapping
(iv) Xenophobic attacks
(v) Rape
(vi) Unemployment; are outcome of deficient societal values. These scenarios are causes from lack of regards for availed resources.

Developed nations are profound with adequate management of resources with high esteem on self-reliance, which is dependency on utility of internal resources for growth and development. Nations that have drastically transformed emphasizes more on utility of internal resources in meeting societal needs. The benefit of self-realism governance is that resources are adequately and optimally put to use, and it guarantees development of all sectors at own pace and creating opportunity of employment for the populace, aiding socio-economic growth, and minimizing social vices.

Classification of Values

Walter Goodnow Everett classified values into the following eight categories;

1. Economic values
2. Bodily values
3. Value of recreation
4. Value of association
5. Character values
6. Aesthetic values
7. Intellectual values
8. Religious values

Everett's classification does not cover all the values in our life. To this we can add political values, social values, legal values, cultural values, moral values, educational values, scholastic values, industrial values, athletic values, values of life, medical values, values of language, technical values and emotional values. Thus, the nature system has many values which constitute the base for the existence of the humans. These values can be classified as follows by their qualities;

1. Individual values and social values
2. Natural values and artificial values
3. Physical values and mental values
4. Instrumental values and intrinsic values
5. Temporary values and permanent values
6. Exclusive values and universal values
7. Lower values and higher values
8. Unproductive values and productive values
9. Active values and inactive values
10. Personal and impersonal values
11. Theoretical values and practical values
12. Relative values and absolute values

Values are indeed manifold and countless, and values in our life are interconnected. Science, education and political activities depend, more or less, on economic values, because we need some degree of economic support for our social life. Conversely, we know that intellectual and political values influence the economy as some remarkable talent or excellent policy can make a home or a nation prosperous.

Hierarchy of Values

M. Scheler (1874-1928) presented the following principles in deciding the rank of values;

First, the longer the value lasts, the higher it is. For example, while the value of pleasure lasts for the duration of the feeling of pleasure, the mental value remains after the disappearance of the circumstances. (timelessness);

Second, the harder it is to reduce the quality of the value as its carrier divides or the harder it is to increase the quality of the value as its carrier enlarges, the higher the value is. For example, while the value of material goods reduces as the goods divide, the value of mental goods is indivisible and not related to the number of people concerned. (indivisibility);

Third, the higher value becomes the base for the lower value. The fewer other values the value has as its base, the higher it is. (independence);

Fourth, there is an intrinsic relationship between the rank of the value and the depth of satisfaction from its realization. In other words, the deeper the satisfaction connected to the value, the higher the value is. For example, the physical satisfaction is strong but shallow. On the contrary, the satisfaction from artistic meditation is a deep experience. The depth of satisfaction is not related to its strength. (depth of satisfaction);

Fifth, the less the sense of the value is related to the existence of its carrier, the higher the value is. For example, the value of pleasure has significance in relation to the sense of sensuality. The value of life exists for those with the sense of life, but the moral value exists absolutely and independently from those who feel it. (absoluteness)

In accordance with the above principles, Scheler classified the values into the following four categories;

1. The value of pleasure and displeasure (the emotional value)
2. The value of the sense of life (welfare as a subsidiary value to it)
3. The mental value (perception, beauty, justice)
4. The value of holiness.

Thus, Scheler suggested five principles, by which the ranks of values can be decided, and presented four levels of values. This idea is very instrumental in deciding the ranks of values. He placed the durable mental values higher than the temporary physical values, put the mental goods higher than the material goods, placed the satisfaction from artistic meditation above the material satisfaction, appreciated the value of the sense of life more highly than the emotional value of pleasure and displeasure, and placed the mental value of perception, beauty, and justice higher than the value of the sense of life. This is an excellent idea that can offer the right sense of values for some contemporary people with the mistaken sense of values.

Scheler's idea of values was succeeded by Nicolai Hartmann (1882-1950). He talked about the relationship between the height and strength of the value. He said that the higher value was weak, but the lower value was strong. The higher value is structurally complex, but the lower value is elementary. Something elementary is strong. The betrayal of the lower value is a more serious sin than the betrayal of the higher value. The realization of the higher value is more valuable than that of the lower value. He arranged values by their height; honesty, integrity, the love of remote people and the virtue of giving by their height. Honesty is the lowest among these and the virtue of giving is the highest. Furthermore, the anti-values corresponding to these values can be illustrated as follows; dishonesty, lie, the lack of love for neighbors, inability for unconditional faith, the lack of love for remote people, the lack of the virtue of giving.

Hartmann's remarks that the higher value is weak and the lower value is strong can be appreciated as grasping values ontologically. This can easily be understood if we get to know his idea of layered existence in which he understood the world in layers and divided the world of existence into four levels, which constituted four layers of existence, (i) the layer of mental existence, (ii) the layer of conscious existence, (iii) the layer of live existence and (iv) the layer of physical existence. In the layer of mental existence are the humans, in the layer of conscious existence are the higher animals, in the layer of live existence are the plants, and in the layer of physical existence are the lifeless things.

(1) The humans include all the four layers of existence in themselves and are understood as concrete objects assembling these in a peculiar way.
(2) The higher animals are the aggregates of the layers of physical, live and conscious existence.
(3) The plants are the aggregates of the layers of physical and live existence.
(4) The lifeless things include only the layer of physical existence.

The layer of physical existence is the lowest but most basic layer of existence on which all the living organisms in the world live. If this layer of physical existence is destroyed, all the living organisms as well as all the precious mental and cultural heritage of the mankind will disappear at the same time. Therefore, the conservation of the layer of physical existence is very important.

Hartmann said that murder was the most serious crime, but more review is required on the act of murder. As for murder, there are the act of individual murder by an offender, the mass destruction of humans by a war, or, in the modern era, the act of annihilating the mankind as well as all the living organisms in the world by nuclear weapons. Considering the destructive power of nuclear weapons held by some countries, which can turn the surface of the earth into ashes, the act of provoking a nuclear war or that of destroying the earth is the most serious crime. Thus, the act of destroying the earth and annihilating the mankind as well as all the living organisms is the most serious crime and the most dreadful anti-value.

The second lowest anti-value is the killing of a number of people by the crime against the state or the nation. The nation states are among the largest organizations made by humans in terms of geographical size or the number of people. The act of a ruler who, by using a large organization as the state, initiates a war and causes the nation to lose its lives and properties and suffer from the loss of the war, is clearly the crime against the nation or the people. To drive the nation toward a war under the pretext of the prosperity for the nation or the state and kill the people of another state is clearly the low anti-value as an act of genocide. In the past, belligerent kings or rulers, who were very good at martial art or military strategy and frequently invaded other states, were often praised as heroes and respected as objects of adoration, but that should be considered the mistaken sense of value. The person who defends the nation and the state from the invasion of another nation or state, is of course a hero and patriot whose patriotism and courage should be highly appreciated.

The third lowest anti-value is the act of murdering a human. The act of murdering or causing a death of human is the act of destroying the life and body of the human and is heavily punishable up to death penalty.

The next is the act of damaging the human body through violence and other means. The act of damaging the life or the body, which is the base for human existence, is clearly the low anti-value.

The low anti-value next to the act of damaging the human body is the act of destroying the public security and order and harming a number of people such as arson, traffic violation, etc. in addition to these, there are numerous immoral crimes including crimes relating to the properties, which are basic and essential for human life, such as theft, fraud, etc.

The above anti-values can be classified into the following six categories by the ranks from the lowest one:

(i) The act of destroying the earth, the act of annihilating the mankind and all the other living organisms

(ii) The act of mass killing of people by initiating a war or committing treason.
(iii) The act of murdering or causing to death a human.
(iv) The act of greatly harming the society.
(v) The act of damaging the body of a human.
(vi) All the other crimes not covered by the above.

On the contrary, if we observe the humans and the society, we cannot ignore the fact that the human has a dual aspect. E. Durkheim (1858-1917), a French positive sociologist, advocated the dual nature of the human. While the human is a selfish being with desires, he (or she) is also a moral, religious being. While the human is a being of sense and sensual thinking, he (or she) is also a moral, religious being. While the human is a being of sense and sensual thinking, he (or she) is also a being of reason and conceptual thinking. There is a confrontation between holiness and filthiness, and there is a duality of the individual and the society. There is a confrontation between selfishness and morals in the human mind. In the society, there are good persons and bad ones, good deeds and crimes, and justice and injustice.

Relevance of Values in Nation Building

Values are derivatives of thoughts and inner desires. It is driven mainly by our beliefs and cultural system. Values are a set of human beliefs upon which characters, behaviors, and general attitudes are built. They are principles, beliefs, and convictions that drive our moral and ethical behaviors. Every human is a product of Nature and Nurture, there are Intrinsic characteristics of human beings that are bad and undesirable by nature. Some of those bad conducts are inborn and are given expressions even in little children. They show aggression and throw tantrums whenever their egoistic desire or selfish inclinations are not met. No one taught them, but it was inborn and inbred. It is called Id in psychology, which is expressed by greediness, selfishness, avarice, and little or no consideration for others.

However, within human DNA also lies the ego and superego. While the ego tends towards the Id, the superego is more considerate and is willing to delay gratifications.

Examples abound of expressions and appetites tamed by the superego within the human psychological make-up. The superego is the element that got nurtured over nature to make humans function in an acceptable form and find expressions in sharing with others, showing kindness, mercy, forgiveness, love, delayed gratification, patience, gratitude, and all those moral values that we all desire to see and receive from others.

Fundamentally, man is created in dignity and with greater value content than animals, owing to the ability to think, create and decipher, however when a man refused to acknowledge his true worth in following principles that govern his status as a preferred entity in creation, the outcome was that of a debased behavioral pattern and conducts.

The hierarchical setup in society is aimed at ensuring correctness and alignment with the law and natural standards, however, what we see is a departure from the norm. Leaders are to live to serve people and be guided by Law. They are now a fundamental shift from those natural principles that govern behavior within acceptable normative standards, the rule of law has become the rule of men. Men made the rules and created a backdoor for escape when they broke and violate the rules. No nation or organization can prosper under such an equation. Without adherence to the law with divine inspiration for normalcy, with every violation of the law, problems are created. When problems are created, only the application of the law can restore it back to normalcy.

In a world where consumerism and materialism have become the norms, and again, given the influence of the corruptive environment over character building, we found that education, which ostensibly is the core of learning has suffered and has been offered on the altar of craze for wealth and other avaricious tendencies.

Values have been thrown out of the window in most social settings, especially in the African space and domain.

When it comes to Nation's building and development, three major components are required to achieve a society, devoid of poor values, poor morality, and poor ethical standards as well as the disenabling environment. These factors are as follows:

1. Infrastructure
2. Education
3. Justice process system

These factors are the bedrock of any civil society that focuses on making human welfare and general well-being a pivotal goal for existence. The interaction of these three (3) produces a strong, viable, and enabling state in most use cases. Where these are lacking, we found that the society or nation will plunge into a state of pariah or it will become so poor showing and displaying the obvious characteristics of a failed state.

Education is central to the creation of the required human capital that will operate in our Justice process system, where rights are preserved, laws are enforced and accountability is entrenched. Without quality manpower with the right competencies, infrastructures cannot be developed, maintained, and sustained for a better life. This is a menace that threatens to sweep the nation because the number of children that are out of school is increasing specifically in Africa. The budget for education in the continent is seemingly becoming criminalized and abysmally low every year. If no credible plan is brought forth to check the pace, more children shall be out of school in coming years. It has been predicted that by 2030, Africa will have about 50% of the young people in the world. When this fact is juxtaposed with weak and moribund infrastructures, poor production capacity, dying industries, ailing economy, an uncertain political climate, poor health system, and wide-scale insecurity, the stage is set for unprecedented chaos and calamitous atmosphere that could be legendary in size and scope.

In identifying the roots and causative agents for poverty in a Nation, the major factors responsible for poverty and misery in nations are as follows:

1. Leadership
2. Culture
3. Institutions
4. Human capital

5. Policy choices (legislature)
6. Entrepreneurship

From the list above, a combination of Leadership + Policy + Culture determines the Human Capital quality, which in turn drives the institutions of any Nation. Human capital also forms the nucleus of the entrepreneurship sector that drives productivity, giving impetus for economic prosperity and political stability.

All the six variables are interdependent and not a single one can be allowed to go out of sync with the rest, the resultant effect of such laxity shall be quickly felt and it reverberates across the rest variables, altering their net contributions to national development and growth in the direction that is undesirable.

If we consider the African continent, most especially black nations, it has become very obvious that lack of good and sincere leadership across all the areas of concerns, be it home, government, religion is very visible. The leaders are themselves, a product of a bad and decimated culture, whose tools of respect are faulty. Parents no longer have the time and moral discipline to instill good values first by example and second by nurturing their children to imbibe and internalize moral principles and learnings that can assist them in molding their life in tune with fundamental principles and ethics such as:

1. Discipline
2. Faith in God and country
3. Patience
4. Hard work
5. Knowledge acquisition
6. Perseverance and endurance
7. Integrity/honesty
8. Selflessness

The absence of these qualities and principles has become the bane of our society. Meanwhile, these principles are what the protestants preached and practiced in the western world and Europe that led to the intervention of many things that improve living and brought the West to become a wealthy nation with overacting dominance in the world. Therefore, what went wrong was a departure from the fundamental principles that govern behaviors, what went wrong was the refusal to obey these divinely inspired laws and apply them to our lives, at home, at school, at market places, at religious centers and of course in government, if this is done, it will become our critical wisdom value and credible platform of exchange for total wellbeing. Finally, if we hope to see improvements, better life, better education, good infrastructures, a trusted justice process/system, credible health deliveries, a safe and secured society, a rebranded national reputation that is respected globally. Commitment to uphold and practice the rule of law and hold ourselves accountable to its ideals and superiority, regardless of who is involved, is the path to national emancipation and liberty, from the dangerous precipice we are currently standing as a people and as a race.

ESTABLISHING SOCIETAL ENLIGHTENMENT TO AID GOOD GOVERNANCE

Society is a reflectance of his people; of what it is made to be by his habitant. Man is the cradle of knowledge, and knowledge forms the cultivation of administering the society. It is needful to note, that behavior is the mediator between man and the society, Akanni (2020). The concept of microcosm illustrates the outcome of the society to be the input of mans' behavior. This, to large measures, actualize behaviors imminent role in society transformation to suit the pattern it chooses to live with. Behaviors are integration of societal values and belief system. It is the ends means of one's interpersonal interaction and a determinant to enlightenment base on exposure to various environmental stimuli that enhances the knowledge and ways of thinking.

Leadership, in any settings, is a product of his findings; and its attributes are factors to effective governance. In the administrative circle, overseeing affairs within organization entails both the formal and informal acquisition of knowledge and skills to appropriate conducts to effect and acquire the desired goals. It is worthy to identify that administration is about adherence to operational ethics to guide conduct during practices, while governance concerns on upholding the rules of law and policies as stipulated in the constitution with undertone of embrace of societal values. While society is liable for integration of values and informal way of impartation, and the obvious fact that values differs with societal alignment, which the normalcy in behavior varies to human perception.

In his book, 'The Rise of the Public in Enlightenment Europe', James Van Hom Melton examines the rise of the public in the eighteenth-century Europe. During the period, the public assumed a new significance as government came to recognize the power of public opinion in political life. Of course, by then, the expansion of print culture had created a new reading and enlightened public. Thus, it became quite evident that government can no longer take the public for granted, in order to ensure that communication gap does not exist between the government and the citizenry, governments around the globe now pay utmost attention to public enlightenment campaigns. This is a deliberate and conscious strategy to duly inform and educate the citizenry as well as share ideas about government policies, plans, activities and programs.

Sometimes, for various reasons, government's actions and programs and policies, which ironically are conceived for the betterment of the citizenry, are often misconstrued by the people. This trend is not unusual in a democracy. It is in order to ensure that government and the citizenry operate on same page that the government places high premium on effective public information management. An integral part of this is public enlightenment campaign. Hence, the coordination of information machinery as a viable enlightenment platform that disseminate crucial public information about government's plans and actions.

The primary goal of the platform is to create awareness and elicit attitudinal transformation towards informing people about government's policies and programs. This is basically done through the production and distribution of relevant information, Education and Enlightenment Communication. Other strategies include public lectures, symposiums, seminars, workshops and advertorials in both print and electronic media.

This is a clear departure from the transmission model which sees communication not as an exchange of ideas but as the mere transmission of messages with or without a purpose. In order words, once a message is transmitted, it does not matter whether the receiver understands it or not. But public enlightenment is more than that. It is not just an event but a transaction which involves a set of actors and activities. Thus, it is better to rely on the sensitization campaign, which recognizes that the sender and receiver of a message through the feedback mechanism are both simultaneously engaged in sending and receiving messages.

However, for the public enlightenment to be effective, relevant target group and the language it understands have to be identified. It is well positioned to organize a more robust sensitization programs on government policies, the operational arrangement whereby its workers function in their places of origin and relate with the people in the language they understand is an appropriate and credible channel. Effective public enlightenment presupposes that the message being passed is clear and accurate. There should be no ambiguity so that it would be easy to comprehend because human beings use and interpret meanings of words differently.

It is, therefore, safe to affirm that public enlightenment is the lifeblood of any society and vital to the activities of both the government and the private sector. It has led to the promotion of positive change; enhance growth, progress, stability and cohesion. It has also projected the people and the state as progressive, civilized and cultured. Similarly, it has helped to reflect back to the government the views, aspirations, doubts, anxieties and hopes of the people about its policies and programs. Government at all levels should identify the indispensability of a good public enlightenment structure as an integral part of governance. It is in doing this that a virile democratic culture could be attained.

Public Enlightenment and Good Governance

Earlier, I stated that the concept of microcosm illustrates the outcome of the society to be the input of mans' behavior. This is affirmative, what makes the society are not the elements, but the people. The values of the people therein make worth out from the elements which determines the status of the society, and so could be said of any establishment, organizational settings, and governmental parastatals. No matter how resourceful any establishment is, without the appropriate knowledgeable and skillful personnel to manned affairs of the organization operations; it will somewhat in the unsystematic pattern of operations due to un-professionalized etiquettes yields to lack of productivity and shortfalls in expected outcome.

Public enlightenment is a priority for the society and to effect good governance. Thus, it is often referred to as dissemination of information to citizenry. But it is actually beyond it. I perceived it as values in two shapes, (i) intelligence and, (ii) morals

(i) **Intelligence:** The concept of intelligence means the acquirement, processing and storage of information. From this point of view, intelligence is restricted to the cognitive, mental abilities of the human being and it is frequently called academic intelligence. This is defined as the intellectual performance, within a closed system, on academic tasks or on academic problems that have fixed goals, a fixed structure, and known elements, and is distinguished from social, everyday, successful, or practical intelligence. Intelligence and competencies are often applied as synonyms. Some distinctive features commonly accepted in the literature are the context-specificity of competence and the more general meaning of intelligence constructs across situations or contexts. Competence appears to be more subject to modification and learning, whereas intelligence is comparatively stable over time and seen as hereditary to a large extent. However, intelligence is often a necessary part of the evaluation of competence.

(ii) **Morals:** The question of morality is the question of identifying the target of moral theorizing. Identifying this target enables us to see different moral theories as attempting to capture the very same thing. There does not seem to be much reason to think that a single definition of morality will be applicable to all mora discussions. One reason for this is that "morality" seems to be used in two distinct broad senses: a descriptive sense and a normative sense. More particularly, the term "morality" can be used either.

- Descriptively to refer to certain codes of conduct put forward by a society or a group (such as a religion), or accepted by an individual for her own behavior, or
- Normatively to refer to a code of conduct that, given specified conditions, would be put forward by all rational people.

If one uses "morality" in its descriptive sense, and therefore uses it to refer to codes of conduct actually put forward by distinct groups or societies, one will almost certainly deny that there is a universal morality that applies to all human beings. The descriptive use of "morality" is the one used by anthropologists when they report on the morality of the societies that they study. Accepting that there are two uses of sense of "morality" – a descriptive sense and a normative sense – does not commit one to holding that the "distinction between descriptions and norms- between what is and what ought to be- is obvious and unbridgeable. That is, it is obvious that one can sensibly describe the moralities of various groups without making any normative claims.

Basic literacy, political education and good governance are fundamental factors that create the basis for awareness and positive transformation in human societies for social and economic development. These developments cut across all essential services that constitute the essential requirements for good living, like the provision of sound education, health care services, security, food, shelter, power supply, environmental safety, etc.

Public education has played strategic role in the sustenance of government policies and programs; therefore, this enables and enriches stake holders in the decisions on how their future is being decided, how their funds are expended, through expressions of their feelings, evaluation of government performance and the need for improvement. This is so because the essence of any form of government worldwide is to improve the living conditions of its citizens through good governance and public accountability. Public enlightenment provides the philosophical basis and model that enable all stakeholders gain access to each other. The objective is to achieve efficient dissemination of information; taking into consideration the geopolitical and socio-economic nature with peculiarities to the nation.

Good Governance is an approach to government that is committed to creating a system founded in justice and peace that protects individual's human rights and civil liberties. According to the United Nations, Good governance is measured by the eight factors of Participation, Rule of Law, Transparency, Responsiveness, Consensus Oriented, Equity and Inclusiveness, Effectiveness and Efficiency, and Accountability.

Features of Good Governance

i. **Participation:** Requires that all groups, particularly those most vulnerable, have direct or representative access to the systems of government. This manifests as a strong civil society and citizens with the freedom of association and expression.

ii. **Rule of Law:** Is exemplified by impartial legal systems that protect the human rights and civil liberties of all citizens, particularly minorities. This is indicated by an independent judicial branch and a police force free from corruption.

iii. **Transparency:** Means that citizens understand and have access to the means and manner in which decisions are made, especially if they are directly affected by such decisions. This information must be provided in an understandable and accessible format, typically translated through the media.

iv. **Responsiveness:** Simply involves that institutions respond to their stakeholders within a reasonable time frame.

v. **Consensus Oriented:** Is demonstrated by an agenda that seeks to mediate between the many different needs, perspectives, and expectations of a diverse citizenry. Decisions needs to be made in a manner that reflects a deep understanding of the historical, cultural, and social context of the community.

vi. **Equity and Inclusiveness:** Depends on ensuring that all members of a community feel included and empowered to improve or maintain their wellbeing, especially those individuals and groups that are the most vulnerable.

vii. **Effectiveness and Efficiency:** Is developed through the sustainable use of resources to meet the needs of a society. Sustainability refers to both ensuring social investments carry through and natural resources are maintained for future generations.

viii. **Accountability:** Refers to institutions being ultimately accountable to the people and one another. This includes government agencies, civil society, and the private sector all being accountable to one another as well.

INFLUENCING NATION BUILDING WITH VALUE ORIENTATION

No nation can be of relevance without strong value system as it forms the integral aspect that appreciates totality of beings regardless of differences. It is a measure to placement of worth in all human endeavors and its impacts weighs much on individual and societal progress.

Behaviors are characterized by influence of values mold, and revolves round two basic principles; which are-

   (i)   The discipline of Teaching; and
   (ii) The discipline of Guidance and Counseling

Both are formalized ways of behavior modification that takes place through strategic system of learning with defined professional procedures that aid the desired outcome of expected behaviors.

   (i)   **Teaching:** is a process that is aid by a teacher, and the quality of knowledge is determined by the teachers' exposure to a specific component of knowledge; coupled with portraying good teaching qualities that made the teaching-learning process stimulating to the students. It can also be referred to as engagement with learners to enable their understanding and application of knowledge, concepts and processes. It includes design, content selection, delivery, assessment and reflection.

To teach is to engage students in learning; thus, teaching consists of getting students involved in the active construction of knowledge. A teacher requires not only knowledge of subject matter, but knowledge of how students learn and how to transform them into active learners. Good teaching, then, requires a commitment to systematic understanding of learning. The aim of teaching is not only to transmit information, but also to transform students from passive recipients of other people's knowledge into active constructors of their own and others' knowledge. The teacher cannot transform without the student's active participation. Teaching is fundamentally about creating the pedagogical, social, and ethical conditions under which students agree to take charge of their own learning, individually and collectively.

Learning can be defined as the process of acquisition of knowledge through a necessitated procedure of studying, and being taught, Akanni (2020).

Assessment can be defined as the measurement of the impart of the teaching-learning process, Akanni (2020).

Teaching as a discipline is knowledge encompassing, broaden in many scopes of life and assumed vast roles in execution of duties beyond what could be perceive. Some of the qualities of a good teacher are:

1. **Good teacher are strong communicators:** By communicating with student with strong communication skills, they will be able to approach the subject in a more enjoyable way that better support their learning.
2. **Good teachers listen well:** Communication doesn't stop when the teacher is done talking. Listening well is one of the most important skills needed to be a teacher. Teachers that are skilled in listening and observing often pick up on what isn't being said, such as in students, skills, confidence levels etc.
3. **Good teachers focus on collaboration:** Working in education means not truly working alone. From paraprofessionals and teaching assistants to other classroom teachers and school leaders,

working as a teacher often means working effectively in a group.

4. **Good teachers are adaptable:** Effective teachers need to be able to work in a constantly evolving environment and adjust their teaching methods based on the age of their students, the resources available and changing curriculum, practices and requirements.
5. **Good teachers are engaging:** Being able to engage students with humor, creative lessons and a strong classroom presence is an important part of what makes someone a good teacher.
6. **Good teachers show empathy:** Another key to engaging students and improving their learning is to treat each student as an individual, by being empathetic and understanding to what may be going on in their lives.
7. **Good teachers have patience:** No matter what grade level you're teaching, your patience will be tested while working as an educator. Whether you're managing classroom behavior, working with colleagues with different views, or communicating student issues or progress with parents, patience is one of the most important skills to practice as a teacher.

8. **Good teachers' value real world learning:** Teachers who bring their students' learning into the real world are often some of the most engaging. But it's important for teachers to bring their own learning into the real world, too.
9. **Good teachers share best practices:** A willingness to share knowledge and experiences with others is one of the most important qualities of a good teacher. Education is a hands-on field and often requires experimentation within the classroom to discover which methods of communicating with students work best. Part of being an effective teacher is sharing your findings and best practices with others in the field.
10. **Good teachers are lifelong learners:** One of the key skills needed to be a good teacher is a dedication to continued education and a love of learning. Whether you're learning more about your subject area, learning new methods of communication or even exploring how to bring more technology into your classroom, continuing to expand your own knowledge is key to expanding that of the students.

These qualities are expected to be indoctrinated in pupils' personality after completion of a successful teaching-learning process designed to instill values to aid individual and societal development.

(ii) **Counseling:** is a process of behavioral adjustment that entails series of information exchange between a disturbed client seeking modification in any aspect of endeavors and a professionally trained counselor endowed with knowledge on how to reach the desired behavioral target, Akanni (2020). The definition contains four key words; behavior, adjustment, modification, and target/objective.

- **Behavior** is any activity that can be observed, recorded and measured. This includes, what living beings or organisms do- that is, their movements in space. It also includes what people say or write. It is a function of the integrative processes of the growth of each child. It is also dependent on his maturational level and experience. Behavior may be described as adient or abient.

    Adient behavior refers to approach behavior or behavior that attracts someone to another or something. For instance, a smile from someone to a child usually attracts the child to that person. Similarly, success in a particular subject would attract the child to that subject and he develops interest in it.

Abient behavior may be regarded as avoidant behavior. This refers to the behavior that leads to someone avoiding, withdrawing or moving away from or fearing to respond favorably to someone or something.

- **Adjustment:** it is a behavioral process by which humans maintain an equilibrium among their various needs or between their needs and obstacles of their environments. A sequence of adjustment begins when a need is felt and ends when it is satisfied. In general, the adjustment process involves four parts: (1) a need or motive in the form of a strong persistent stimulus, (2) the thwarting or nonfulfillment of this need, (3) varied activity, or exploratory behavior accompanied by problem solving, and (4) some response that removes or at least reduces the initiating stimulus and completes the adjustment.
- **Target behavior:** It is the specific behavior selected for change. That means behavior selected for change, are not selected at random. It is the behavior that are immediately necessary and necessary for long-term success that are selected for change.

Counseling is a standardized procedure where clients' unpleasant behaviors are processed and examined through a heart to heart interaction with the aim of proffering permanent resolution through possible recommendation that ameliorate the problem. It is human eccentric and revolves on behavior modification.

Behavior Modification

Brown et al (1971) say behavior modification is a behavioral science technique which involves the application of principles derived from research in experimental psychology to alleviate human suffering and increase human functioning.

The troubles that clients bring to counselors are so complex that, it is difficult to see any system of help as "an elegant solution. Behavior modification is now seen as a process of helping people to learn how to solve certain interpersonal, emotional, and decision problems. The key word in the definition is "learn." Counselors are people who help their client to learn. They are in the education business as well as teachers, school administrators, psychologists, mental health workers and social workers. All these occupations, have in common the goal of producing changes in the behavior of clients.

Basic Principles of Behavior Modification

The basic principles on which behavior modification revolves are:

(1) All behaviors are learned by conditioning in the environment. Learning is inferred from a subject's behavior.
(2) Behavior is a function of the interaction of hereditary and environmental variables
(3) Maladaptive behavior is learned and can be unlearned according to the same principles as adaptive behavior. Changes in behavior can be brought by systematic and gradually introduced changes in the environment.
(4) Behavior modifiers are concerned with specific, precise and current problems.
(5) A number of techniques can be applied in behavior modification; such as reinforcement, modeling, role-play stimulation and counterconditioning.

Essential Features of Behavior Modification

Four interrelated characteristics of the approach enable behavior modifiers to respond flexibly and adopt continuously improving procedures to help their clients.

(1) Criteria for formulating Counselling Goals

When a counselling goal is finally formulated in behavior modification, it must meet three criteria:

i. It must be a goal desired by the client,
ii. The counselor must be willing to help the client achieve this goal;
iii. It must be possible to assess the extent to which the client achieves the goal.

(2) Tailoring techniques to the Client

Behavior modifiers do not use the same technique with every client. They try to select a procedure or combination of procedures most likely to help a client accomplish his particular goals.

(3) Experimenting with procedures

The systematic testing of many procedures and variations on those procedures is necessary so that the profession can develop those techniques best suited for helping various kinds of clients.

(4) Improving Procedures on the Basic of Relevant Evidence

While on the other hand;

Guidance: Appropriate rightful application of behavior in meeting desired objective, Akanni (2020). It facilitates people throughout their lives to manage their own educational, training, occupational, personal, social, and life choices so that they reach their full potential and contribute to the development of a better society.

Principles of Guidance

1. **Principle of all-round development of the individual:**
   Guidance must take into account the all-round development of the individual when bringing about desirable adjustment in any particular area of his personality.

2. **The principle of human uniqueness:**
   No two individuals are alike. Individuals differ in their physical, mental, social, and emotional development. Guidance service must recognize these differences and guide each individual according to their specific need.

3. **Principle of holistic development:**
   Guidance has to be imparted in the context of total development of personality. The child grows as a whole and even if one aspect of personality is in focus, the other areas of development which are indirectly influencing the personality have also to be kept in mind.

4. **The principle of cooperation:**
   No individual can be forced into guidance. The consent and cooperation of the individual is a pre-requisite for providing guidance.
5. **The principle of continuity:**
   Guidance should be regarded as a continuous process of service to an individual in different stages of his life.
6. **The principle of extension:**
   Guidance service should not be limited to a few persons, who give observable evidence of its need, but it should be extended to all persons of all ages, who can benefit from it directly or indirectly.
7. **The principle of elaboration:**
   Curriculum materials and teaching procedures should be elaborated according to view point of guidance.
8. **The principle of adjustment:**
   While it is true that guidance touches every aspect of an individual's life, it is chiefly concerned with an individual's physical or mental health, with his adjustment at home, school, society and vocation.
9. **Principle of individual needs:**

The individual and his needs are of utmost significance. Recognition of individual freedom, worth, respect, and dignity is the hallmark of guidance. Freedom to make a choice and take a decision needs to be respected and encouraged.

10. The principle of expert opinion:
Specific and serious guidance problems should be referred to persons who are trained to deal with particular area of adjustment for their opinion.

11. The principle of evaluation:
The guidance programme should be evaluated in terms of its effectiveness and improvement. Evaluation is essential for the formulation of new goals or re-drafting the existing goals.

12. The principle of responsibility:
Parents and teachers have great responsibility in the execution of the work of guidance. The responsibility for guidance should be centered on a qualified and trained person, who is the head of the guidance center.

13. The principle of periodic appraisal:
Periodic appraisal should be made of the existing guidance programme so that requisite changes, if any can be carried out for its improvement.

As a human-centric profession, counselling consists of three therapeutic approaches. Each offering their own way of working and ideas about human actions. Some counselors work 'eclectically', drawing on many models, whilst others work 'integratively', blending two or more types. When people attend counseling sessions, the difference is whether it's 'directive' (where the counselor may suggest actions and exercises) or 'non-directive' (where the individual take the lead). It's not possible to look at all types, but three common approaches are summarized:

i. **Psychodynamic:** Based on the idea that our past has a bearing on our present feelings and important relationships (possibly from childhood), and may be recounted with others in later life. The counselor aims to be neutral, giving little information about themselves, making it likely that these relationships will be echoed in the individual by assisting through the difficulties. This type is non-directive

ii. **Person-centered:** Based on the principle of the counselor providing three therapeutic 'core-conditions':

- Empathy (imagining yourself in someone's position)
- Unconditional position regard (warm and positive feelings regardless of behavior)

- Congruence (openness and honesty).

Here the relationship developed is a means of healing and change., which are non-directive.

    iii. **Cognitive-behavioral therapy (CBT):** Concerned with the way people's beliefs shape their interpretation of experience. Its aim is to change irrational or self-defeating beliefs and behaviors by altering negative ways of thinking. The counselor might provide tasks to do between sessions that monitor emotional upsets to see what triggers them, looking for evidence for and against these thoughts, and encouraging people to think in a less negative way. This type is directive.

Counseling specializes on maintaining and shaping societal behavioral expectation; the eccentric nature of the profession with endowed knowledge in virtually all human facets makes the discipline a requisite to be integrated in any pattern of administrative system for guidance in the conduct of activities to attain utmost performance and effectiveness in leadership roles. The impart of counselors in development of any human endeavors is comprehensive as the roles it plays in providing adequate information is beyond measures and can be compare to non. And it banks on three principles of information availability, which are:

(i) Validity of information: is referred to as the information necessary for system construction, model assessment and testing, and guiding the system experiments to solve the difficulty is sufficient and accurate.

(ii) Reliability of information: is the probability that information about the state of the environment correctly identifies the environment as being in state, and defined over the range.

(iii) Usability of information: refers to information that accurately applies specific system of operation.

These quantifies the effectiveness and application of availed information during communication, as information is processed in a strategic pattern to suit the issue it is being provided for.

CONCLUSION

Nation building should not be perceived as a boarden on leadership but rather should be regarded a collective responsibility of the people within the confined space for good governance to flourish. This weighs much on societal roles in establishing and fostering values that aids the developmental pattern of the people into becoming more responsive in action towards the environment with respective contribution expressed from a sense of belonging and togetherness in reaching common objectives. This, thus far, cannot be established without a strong societal value system, well-structured teaching learning process, and guidance and counselling procedure that check and balances activities in domains of behavioral formulation.

The role of a structured learning system is essential in sustaining peace in any society as it places worth in all societal endeavors, which can be proven to be the drive to growth in developed nations. The structural establishments of the knowledge encompassing programmes and value orientation system are designed in pattern that synchronizes the aforementioned behavioral formulation domains into an institutionalize system that impart requisite knowledge and expected behavior required for effective leadership and citizenry.

References

E.A Akinade, and V.O Adedipe(2004). Behaviour Modification, Principles and Practices

Munroe, M. (2003). The Power of Character in Leadership.

Ogunsanwo, O. (2009). AWO, Unfinished Greatness.

Conference Proceeding, (2007). Counselling Association Of Nigeria Journal.

Conference Proceed, (2020), Paperwork Presentation. Counselling Association Of Nigeria.

Puja Mondal. Social Stratification: Meaning, Types, and Characteristic | Sociology.

Princewill Ene. Public Policy | Definition, Characteristics, Types & Theories.

Princewill Ene. Citizenship, Definition & Method of Acquiring Citizenship.

Tong-Keun Min./Chung Nam National University. Philosophy of Values | A study on the Hierarchy of Values.

Prof. Pat Utomi. Why Nations are Poor.

Stanford Encyclopedia of Philosophy – The Definition of Morality (2020).

John Parakimalil – Scope of Guidance / Principles of Guidance.

David A. Wilson. Nation Building and Revolutionary War (1962)

Wim Laven, In Encyclopedia of Violence, Peace, & Conflict (Third Edition 2022).

French Revolution
https://www.history.com/topics/france/french-revolution

http://www.toppr.com/guides/business-economics/introduction-to-business-economics/socialist-economy

Made in the USA
Middletown, DE
13 March 2024